THE PENGUIN POETS

POETRY OF THE THIRTIES

POETRY
OF THE THIRTIES

*

INTRODUCED AND EDITED BY
ROBIN SKELTON

PENGUIN BOOKS

Penguin Books Ltd, Harmondsworth, Middlesex, England
Penguin Books, 625 Madison Avenue, New York, New York 10022, U.S.A.
Penguin Books Australia Ltd, Ringwood, Victoria, Australia
Penguin Books Canada Ltd, 2801 John Street, Markham, Ontario, Canada L3R 1B4
Penguin Books (N.Z.) Ltd, 182-190 Wairau Road, Auckland 10, New Zealand

—

Published in Penguin Books 1964
Reprinted 1967, 1969, 1971 (twice), 1975, 1977, 1979, 1980

—

Copyright © Robin Skelton, 1964
All rights reserved

—

Set, printed and bound in Great Britain
by Cox & Wyman Ltd, Reading
Set in Monotype Baskerville

Contents

ACKNOWLEDGEMENTS   11

INTRODUCTION   13

A NOTE ON THE TEXTS USED   39

I. IN OUR TIME

Louis MacNeice : Autumn Journal, III   45

W. H. Auden : Song for the New Year   47

C. Day Lewis : The Magnetic Mountain   49

Stephen Spender : An Elementary School Class Room in a Slum   51

Kenneth Allott : The Children   52

Michael Roberts : In Our Time   53

W. H. Auden : A Communist to Others   54

Rex Warner : Hymn   59

C. Day Lewis : The Magnetic Mountain   61

Julian Bell : Nonsense   62

C. Day Lewis : The Magnetic Mountain   63

William Empson : Just a Smack at Auden   64

Edgar Foxall : A Note on Working-Class Solidarity   66

Gavin Ewart : Audenesque for an Initiation   67

C. Day Lewis : Newsreel   69

Clere Parsons : Different   70

W. H. Auden : O for Doors to be Open   70

Louis MacNeice : Bagpipe Music   72

William Empson : Missing Dates   73

John Betjeman : Slough   74

Francis Scarfe : Beauty, Boloney   76

Randall Swingler : From *The New World This Hour Begets*   77

Stephen Spender : The Express   79

Louis MacNeice : Birmingham   80

CONTENTS

Stephen Spender : The Landscape near an Aerodrome 82
Anne Ridler : At Richmond 83
Charles Madge : Instructions, V 83
Francis Scarfe : Progression 84
C. Day Lewis : The Bells that Signed 85
W. H. Auden : Poems, XII 86
H. B. Mallalieu : Two Preludes 87
Robert Hamer : Torch Song 88
Rex Warner : Sonnet 89
Stephen Spender : Easter Monday 89
Stephen Spender : New Year 90

II. THE LANDSCAPE WAS THE OCCASION

Anne Ridler : Zennor 95
Michael Roberts : The Secret Springs 95
Ruthven Todd : In September 97
Louis MacNeice : Poem 98
Geoffrey Parsons : Europe a Wood 99
Stephen Spender : The Pylons 99
C. Day Lewis : From Feathers to Iron, 14 100
Rex Warner : Sonnet 101
Peter Hewitt : Place of Birth 102
Bernard Gutteridge : Home Revisited 104
Bernard Spencer : Allotments : April 105
Anne Ridler : Aisholt Revisited 106

III. TO WALK WITH OTHERS

Stephen Spender : I Think Continually 111
Kenneth Allott : Lament for a Cricket Eleven 112
C. Day Lewis : A Carol 113
John Short : Carol 114
Michael Roberts : The Child 114
F. T. Prince : The Token 115
John Betjeman : Death of King George V 115

CONTENTS

John Pudney: Resort   116

Geoffrey Grigson: Reginal Order   116

William Empson: To an Old Lady   117

John Betjeman: On a Portrait of a Deaf Man   118

Ronald Bottrall: Epitaph for a Riveter   119

Vernon Watkins: The Collier   119

John Betjeman: Death in Leamington   121

Dylan Thomas: In Memory of Ann Jones   122

Bernard Spencer: Part of Plenty   123

Louis MacNeice: The British Museum Reading Room   124

Geoffrey Grigson: And Forgetful of Europe   125

Norman Cameron: Public-House Confidence   127

John Betjeman: In Westminster Abbey   127

Edgar Foxall: Sea Dirge   129

IV. AND I REMEMBER SPAIN

W. H. Auden: Spain   133

John Cornford: Full Moon at Tierz   137

Charles Madge: The Times   139

Kenneth Allott: Prize for Good Conduct   140

Bernard Spencer: A Thousand Killed   141

Edgar Foxall: Poem ('He awoke from dreams . . .')   142

Geoffrey Grigson: The Non-Interveners   142

Bernard Spencer: A Cold Night   143

Stephen Spender: Two Armies   144

John Cornford: To Margot Heinemann   146

Stephen Spender: Port Bou   146

Stephen Spender: Ultima Ratio Regum   148

Laurie Lee: A Moment of War   149

Stephen Spender: Thoughts During an Air Raid   150

John Cornford: A Letter from Aragon   151

Laurie Lee: Music in a Spanish Town   152

Laurie Lee: Words Asleep   153

Dylan Thomas: The Hand that Signed the Paper   153

Stephen Spender: Fall of a City   154

George Barker : Elegy on Spain   155
Louis MacNeice : Autumn Journal, VI   160

V. AS FOR OURSELVES

W. H. Auden : To a Writer on His Birthday   167
Louis MacNeice : Autumn Journal, XV   170
John Betjeman : Distant View of a Provincial Town   172
Norman Cameron : Forgive me, Sire   173
H. B. Mallalieu : Lament for a Lost Life   174
Rex Warner : Light and Air   176
Geoffrey Parsons : Suburban Cemetery   178
F. T. Prince : An Epistle to a Patron   179
Bernard Spencer : Evasions   183
William Empson : Reflection from Anita Loos   184
Dylan Thomas : I Have Longed to Move Away   185
George Barker : Resolution of Dependence   186
Clifford Dyment : The Pharos   188
Julian Symons : Poem ('If truth can still be told . . .')   188
Randall Swingler : Request for the Day   189
W. H. Auden : The Dream   190
W. H. Auden : Lay Your Sleeping Head   191
Louis MacNeice : Meeting Point   192
Norman Cameron : To a Greedy Lover   193
Norman Cameron : In the Queen's Room   194
William Empson : Aubade   194
Vernon Watkins : Elegy on the Heroine of Childhood   196
William Empson : This Last Pain   198
C. Day Lewis : The Conflict   199
William Empson : Homage to the British Museum   200
W. H. Auden : Poems, XXX   201
Randall Swingler : In Death the Eyes are Still   202
Norman Cameron : No Remedy   202
W. H. Auden : May with its Light Behaving   203
C. Day Lewis : The Magnetic Mountain, 24   204
Louis MacNeice : An Eclogue for Christmas   205

VI. WHEN LOGICS DIE

Kenneth Allott : Offering   213

Philip O'Connor : Poem ('The clock ticks on . . .')   215

Ruthven Todd : Worm Interviewed   215

Dylan Thomas : And Death Shall Have No Dominion   216

Rayner Heppenstall : Risorgimento   217

David Gascoyne : Figure in a Landscape   218

Dylan Thomas : Light Breaks Where No Sun Shines   221

David Gascoyne : Morning Dissertation   222

Geoffrey Grigson : Three Evils   223

Philip O'Connor : 'Blue Bugs in Liquid Silk'   223

Geoffrey Grigson : Before a Fall   224

Dylan Thomas : Twenty-four Years Remind the Tears of My Eyes   225

Hugh Sykes Davies : From *Petron* ('In the midst of a ravaged city . . .')   226

Hugh Sykes Davies : From *Petron* ('A spider weaves his web . . .')   226

Hugh Sykes Davies : Poem ('In the stump of the old tree . . .')   227

Dylan Thomas : The Force that Through the Green Fuse   228

David Gascoyne : And the Seventh Dream is the Dream of Isis   229

Philip O'Connor : Useful Letter   232

David Gascoyne : The Very Image   234

Roger Roughton : Soluble Noughts and Crosses   235

Dylan Thomas : I see the Boys of Summer . . .   237

Roger Roughton : Animal Crackers in Your Croup   239

Roger Roughton : Lady Windermere's Fan-Dance   240

Dylan Thomas : Should Lanterns Shine   241

Philip O'Connor : Poems 5–11 ('Captain Busby . . .')   242

VII. HAIR BETWEEN THE TOES

W. H. Auden : The Witnesses   249

Roy Fuller : End of a City   255

CONTENTS

Louis MacNeice : Christina   256
Norman Cameron : The Compassionate Fool   257
Geoffrey Parsons : The Inheritor   258
W. H. Auden : Ballad   259
Charles Madge : Delusions, II   260
Roy Fuller : Centaurs   261
John Lehmann : This Excellent Machine   262
Michael Roberts : The Caves   263
Ruthven Todd : Time Was My Friend   264
Ruthven Todd : Dictator   265
Christopher Caudwell : The Progress of Poetry   265
Ruthven Todd : God the Holy Ghost   266
Norman Cameron : The Disused Temple   267
Ruthven Todd : Apotheosis of Hero   268
Norman Cameron : The Unfinished Race   268
David Gascoyne : Sonnet   269
Ruthven Todd : A Fable   269

VIII. FAREWELL CHORUS

Louis MacNeice : The Sunlight on the Garden   273
Henry Reed : Hiding Beneath the Furze   274
Ruthven Todd : It was Easier   275
Louis MacNeice : Prognosis   277
Louis MacNeice : London Rain   278
W. H. Auden : September 1, 1939   280
David Gascoyne : Farewell Chorus   283

INDEX OF AUTHORS   289
INDEX OF TITLES   297

Acknowledgements

For permission to publish poems in this anthology, acknowledgement is made to the following: for Kenneth Allott to the author; for W. H. Auden to the author and Faber & Faber Ltd; for George Barker to Faber & Faber Ltd; for Julian Bell to The Hogarth Press; for John Betjeman to John Murray Ltd; for Ronald Bottrall to Sidgwick & Jackson Ltd; for Norman Cameron to The Hogarth Press Ltd; for Christopher Caudwell to Lawrence & Wishart Ltd; for John Cornford to Christopher Cornford and Jonathan Cape Ltd; for Clifford Dyment to J. M. Dent Ltd; for William Empson to Chatto & Windus Ltd; for Gavin Ewart to the author; for Roy Fuller to André Deutsch Ltd; for David Gascoyne to the author; for Geoffrey Grigson to the author; for Bernard Gutteridge to the author; for Rayner Heppenstall to the author; for Peter Hewitt to the author; for Laurie Lee to The Hogarth Press Ltd; for John Lehmann to David Higham Associates Ltd; for C. Day Lewis to Jonathan Cape Ltd; for Louis MacNeice to Faber & Faber Ltd; for Charles Madge to Faber & Faber Ltd; for Philip O'Connor to the author; for Clere Parsons to Sonia Hambourg; for Geoffrey Parsons to the author; for F. T. Prince to Faber & Faber Ltd; for John Pudney to the author; for Henry Reed to Jonathan Cape Ltd; for Anne Ridler to the author; for Michael Roberts to Faber & Faber Ltd; for Roger Roughton to Mrs Helen Woodyatt; for Francis Scarfe to the author; for John Short to the author; for Bernard Spencer to the author; for Stephen Spender to Faber & Faber Ltd; for Hugh Sykes Davies to the author; for Julian Symons to the author; for Dylan Thomas to J. M. Dent Ltd; for Ruthven Todd to the author and J. M. Dent Ltd; for Rex Warner to the author and The Bodley Head; for Vernon Watkins to Faber & Faber Ltd.

The editor and publishers of *Poetry of the Thirties* have made every effort to trace the copyright holders of poems included in this anthology, but in some cases this has not proved possible. The publishers therefore wish to thank the authors or copyright holders of those poems which are included without acknowledgement above.

Introduction

Even before they were quite over, the thirties took on the appearance of myth; the poets themselves, looking back upon the events of those years, saw heroes and dragons in dramatic perspectives, and many of them uttered suitable valedictory sentiments. It is rare for a decade to be so self-conscious. This in itself makes the study of the poetry of the period interesting, for so many gestures are deliberately 'placed' in the period that it is often hard to tell whether a poem is to be condemned for undergraduate and narcissistic posturing, or praised as a truly witty impersonation of the *Zeitgeist* made more subtle by ironic overtones. Is the 'ham' really ham, or a kind of burlesque? This is a particularly difficult question to answer, as burlesque was a favourite device of the poets of the thirties, as also was apparently 'straight' melodrama. It is not always easy to separate the one from the other.

Problems of this kind can, perhaps, only be solved by arranging the poems of the period alongside one another in such a way that comparisons can be made. This anthology is, in part, an attempt at just such an arrangement, and to that extent must be regarded as a kind of critical essay, for the act of selection and of arrangement is also an act of judgement. Nevertheless, it has not been my intention to use the anthology primarily as a vehicle for my own views of the period; whatever judgements may emerge have emerged naturally during the process of trying to present as objective a record of thirties poetry as possible. To do this I had to decide what material could properly come under the heading 'Thirties'. I decided that anything first printed in a book or periodical between 1 January 1930 and 31 December 1939 could be used. I also decided that any poem

13

appearing in a book in 1940 could reasonably be supposed to have been written during the 1930s and could therefore be included. These limitations were not sufficient by themselves, however. It seemed necessary to define a 'Thirties generation' as well as a 'Thirties period', otherwise the anthology might confuse the picture by including poems written from a different viewpoint by Victorians and Georgians. This 'Thirties generation', once the concept is admitted, almost defines itself. If we take Auden, Day Lewis, Spender, and MacNeice as central figures, we find that the eldest of these was born in 1904. If we look for the youngest poet of any weight to publish a first collection before 1940, we come upon David Gascoyne, who was born in 1916. No younger poet can be said to belong as clearly to the period; indeed, most poets born between 1914 and 1916 first made their impact during the forties. I must admit that 1904 is a more arbitrary date; nevertheless, those poets born between 1900 and 1904 do, on the whole, appear to be writing from a slightly different vantage point from those born only a few years later.

It is easy to see possible explanations for this, though it is dangerous to be too dogmatic. On the face of it, however, it does appear that a man born between 1904 and 1916 differs from anyone born even slightly earlier in having had no real experience of the pre-war period, which was so different from the post-war as to appear almost like a different civilization. The men of the 1904–16 generation were not only deprived of the easy Georgian days, but also pitch-forked into a period of intense social tension in which to do their growing up. The older thirties men struggled through their adolescence during the last days of a war and the early confusions of an embittered peace, while the younger ones were adolescents at the time of the General Strike and the Depression. It was not possible to avoid being affected by these matters, however secure one's own personal life might be. Chartism and the Crimean War left many members of the community completely untouched, but the Great War and the Depression left their mark on every inch of the country. If we make the generally accepted assumption that the years of childhood and adolescence are of fundamental importance to a poet's outlook and development, it does seem reasonable to regard the poets born between 1904 and 1916 as forming some kind of coherent 'poetic generation'. Certainly, it looks as if all these poets *ought* to find themselves with similar attitudes of mind. Life is rarely as neat as the theories which emanate from it, however, and we would do well to be suspicious of anyone who detects absolute uniformity of approach. Nevertheless, as one reads the poetry written by members of this generation, especially that printed between 1930 and 1935, one becomes more and more astonished by the narrow range of its attitudes. Some of this is due to the dominating influence of Auden and his friends. Much of it derives from the apparent wish of so many writers to be part of a 'movement'. A good deal of it can also be explained by the overriding effect of certain key images which are not merely a part of the poetry of the time, but related to current social obsessions. One of these images is that of war.

In *New Country* (1933) Michael Roberts went some way towards identifying the thirties generation in terms similar to ours. In his introduction to this violently propagandist collection of essays, stories, and poems, he wrote:

To me, 'pre-war' means only one sunny market-day at Sturminster Newton, the day I boldly bought a goat for 1s. 9d. and then, shelving all transport problems (we lived thirty miles away) and postponing the announcement to my father, went out into the country and, finding a gatepost for a table, cut out from the *Express* a picture of a dozen Serbian soldiers (we spelt it Servian then) in spotless uniforms, elbow to elbow in a shallow trench, standing exactly like my own toy soldiers, the Royal West Kent Regiment ('The Buffs'), manufactured by Wm. Brittain and Sons Ltd.

But there are others who have even less than a one-and-nine-penny goat for their share of pre-war prosperity; Mr Plomer is older, but most of the contributors to this book are younger, than I. Sergeants of our school O.T.C.s, admirers of our elder brothers, we grew up under the shadow of war: we have no memory of pre-war prosperity and a settled Europe. To us that tale is text-book history . . .

Michael Roberts was born in 1902, and I have made him the only exception to the rule that the poets in this anthology should have been born between 1904 and 1916. He did so much to identify the intellectual *élite* for a great number of people in his anthologies *New Signatures* (1932), *New Country* (1933), and *The Faber Book of Modern Verse* (1936) that he could hardly be omitted from the roll call of Thirties' Men, and his own poems have more in common with those of other poets of the thirties than with most of the work published in the late twenties. His character as a spokesman is also valuable to us, for he writes as a representative of a group rather than as a lonely commentator. It is in this role that, later, in his introduction to *New Country*, he explains his Socialist convictions, and goes on to say:

And by social communism I do not mean any diminution or mystical loss of personal identity or any vague sentiment of universal brotherhood: I mean that extension of personality and consciousness which comes sometimes to a group of men when they are working together for some common purpose.
I think some men had just such an experience in the war, and to them it almost seemed to justify the filth and inhumanity of war. It is something rare in our competing, individualist world, and for myself I can point to only one definite example: a fort-night of wind and heavy snowstorm in the Jura when a dozen of us, schoolboys and undergraduates, came to accept each other's faults and virtues as part of the scheme of things, natural as the weather. I don't think I had any love or personal feeling for them at all: we were, for the moment, part of something a little bigger than ourselves. Impatience and fatigue and personal delight and suffering disappeared, and I remember only, at the end of each

day's work, standing at nightfall on the last spur of the ridge, counting the tiny figures moving down the slope in sight of food and warmth again: nine, ten, eleven, black dots against the snow, and knowing that again the party was complete, uninjured, tired and content.

Here war is approached with something of the same feeling as that expressed by Rupert Brooke, when he wrote of turning

> as swimmers into cleanness leaping,
> Glad from a world grown old and cold and weary. . . .

The same note is heard in Rex Warner's *Hymn*.

> Come then, companions. This is the spring of blood,
> heart's hey-day, movement of masses, beginning of good.

This expression of youth's eager rebelliousness is very similar to that opening Brooke's sonnet:

> Now, God be thanked Who has matched us with His hour,
> And caught our youth, and wakened us from sleeping. . . .

Warner was writing of the Revolution and not of war, of course, but, like Brooke, and like many in their two generations, he found the notion of a social upheaval which should cleanse the country of pettiness and selfishness immensely invigorating. In notions of war and of revolution both saw merely personal anxieties dwarfed by larger and more noble concerns. The great thing about revolution and about war is their communal quality. For Michael Roberts it seems almost that war can be some kind of communal sacrament – the suffering being a part of the spiritual purification necessary for the achieving of the holy condition of absolute togetherness. In many poems of the early thirties the threats directed at the *bourgeoisie* are rather of this kind: the *bourgeois* must expect the penance to hurt a little before he can enjoy the state of blessedness. It is difficult to avoid attaching labels like 'Guilt Complex', 'Masochism', 'Puritanism' to much of this material, just as it is also hard to sympathize with the continual expressions of yearning for that kind of community spirit which we now tend to associate only with second-rate war movies and old-fashioned school stories. Nevertheless, we must realize that mass movements were in the air of the time, and quite explicably. Hunger Marchers were out in England. The militant unemployed were reading the *Daily Worker* (founded in 1930). There was a need and a clamour for social justice. It was easy, indeed, to see society in terms of a class war, and to regard this struggle, not merely in orthodox Marxist terms, but also in terms of the manoeuvres of the School O.T.C. There is, in point of fact, something curiously adolescent in the use of phrases like 'The Enemy', 'The Struggle', and 'The Country', and in the deployment of such words as 'Leader', 'Conspiracy', 'Frontier', 'Maps', 'Guns', and 'Armies' in much of the writing of the period. The poets were, much to their embarrassment, and almost to a man, members of the *bourgeoisie*, and mostly products of public schools, and this may be one reason why almost all their images of communal experience can be so easily translated into terms of the undergraduate reading or climbing party. War was a talking-point for everyone of whatever class during the early thirties, however. A recent boom in war-books had coincided with an equally lively boom in anti-war activities. Articles were being written about 'the next war', and rearmament and disarmament were both being canvassed.

This is not the place to discuss yet again the peace movements, economic theories, political conferences, and debates of the thirties, but to try to identify the main characteristics of the poetry of the time. One of these is the obsession with ideas of community, and another is the obsession with the notion of war. The Spanish Civil War usefully combined both these interests. Although the

Republican Government was not at first Communist-dominated, the rebellion of the generals could be seen as the attack of reactionary capitalism upon progressive socialism. The Spanish Civil War was a symbol become reality; it embodied the class struggle, and also the struggle of the artists against the philistines (did not the Fascists murder Lorca? Was not Picasso on the side of the Government?) Apart from its appeal to the poets, it had also the importance of being something of a political test-case. It could be said, indeed, that, for the intelligentsia, the Second World War came as something of an anticlimax after the Spanish affair.

The Spanish War certainly caught the poets' imaginations. Many joined the International Brigade. It seemed *de rigueur* to visit Spain, and to lend one's name, if not always one's armed presence, to the cause of the workers. Auden and Spender both made visits, the former as a stretcher bearer, the latter as head of English broadcasting in a radio station which he found to be defunct. As the war continued more and more people were confused and disillusioned by the muddles, the lies, and the waste. The Communists appeared more intent upon the destruction of the Anarchists and Trotskyites than on that of the Fascists, and it was clear that, far from being a struggle for democratic liberties, the civil war had become a military training ground for the Axis powers, and a pageant of propaganda for the Communists. Nevertheless, in the early months before disillusion set in, many courageous young men died, among them Christopher Caudwell, Julian Bell, and John Cornford, the last named being only twenty-one, while in England the left-wing *avant-garde* was continually stirred by the reports coming back from the battlefields, the tales of atrocities and heroism, all highly coloured, and many, as Arthur Koestler and Claud Cockburn have since told us, pure fabrications. The degree of excitement can to some extent be judged by the advertisements printed in the *avant-garde* and left-wing Press asking for arms for Spain. *Contemporary Poetry and Prose* in September 1936 devoted the whole of its back cover to the injunction 'Support the Spanish People against Fascism'. The same legend appeared on the next issue, and the issue for November asked readers to 'Support all meetings and demonstrations to end the farce of "non-intervention"'. The last two issues of the magazine simply carried the words ARMS FOR SPAIN on the back cover, and the Editor's announcement of the closure of the magazine read: 'This is the last number of *Contemporary Poetry and Prose* as the Editor is going abroad for some time.'

This final number of *Contemporary Poetry and Prose* appeared in Autumn 1937, and it is instructive to compare its attitude towards the Spanish War with the mood of a full-page display in the March 1938 issue of *New Verse*. This page, surrounded by a black border, read:

1914 – 1938

BE WARNED

BY RUPERT BROOKE

*

In 1913 and 1914 Rupert Brooke declared:

I want to walk 1,000 miles, and write 1,000 plays, and sing 1,000 poems, and drink 1,000 pots of beer, and kiss 1,000 girls, and – oh, a million things.

May 1913

All I want is life in a cottage, and leisure to write supreme poems and plays.

March 1914

I want to live in a hut by a river and pretend I'm Polynesian.

April 1914

I'm so uneasy – subconsciously. All the vague perils of the time – the world seems so dark – and I'm vaguely frightened.

July 1914

But there's a ghastly sort of apathy over half the country and I really think large numbers of male people don't want to die – which is odd. I've been praying for a German air raid.

Xmas 1914

Are you wiser than Rupert Brooke?

*

Winston Churchill delivered a funeral oration over Brooke in *The Times*. The Old Fury is still under age for a funeral oration about you.

TAKE CARE

Apart from doubting Sir Winston's reliability as a prophet, many thirties men appear to have felt that the war was the wrong one. It was a capitalist and imperialist affair; dog was eating dog; it was not a class struggle at all. Fascism was evil, certainly, but so was capitalism. The left-wing writers were not at all happy over it and their unhappiness was not decreased when the Hitler–Stalin pact was made, and Germany and the Soviet Union proceeded to carve up Poland between them. Nevertheless, old habits soon asserted themselves. It might not be the right struggle. It might not be a product of the mass-movement towards the Socialist World State. It *was*, however, a struggle of some sort, and a test. It is characteristic of the thirties that the poets (with the rather embarrassing exception of Auden, who had already begun his career as an American) entered the war against Hitler as evangelists entering, and exhorting others to enter, a somewhat purgatorial moral gymnasium.

Such generalizations as these are, of course, extremely superficial, and must irritate any member of the thirties generation who reads them. Nevertheless, there is a certain appropriateness in prefacing this anthology with one or two large gestures, for most of those made by the self-appointed leaders of the poetic *avant-garde* from 1930 to 1939 were equally pontifical. Again it is useful to turn to Michael

Roberts's *New Country* of 1933, in which he says firmly 'I think, and the writers in this book obviously agree, that there is only one way of life for us: to renounce that system now and to live by fighting against it.' Geoffrey Grigson, in reviewing *New Country*, complained, 'Roberts in a long preface "usses" and "ours" as though he were G.O.C. a new Salvation Army or a cardinal presiding over a Propaganda.'

Grigson's comment could be applied to many articles and poems of the time. The didacticism is earnestly moral, thoroughly evangelical, and indisputably authoritative. It is also, not infrequently, rather naïve. C. Day Lewis, who was the most assiduous propagandist for poetry in the service of socialism, and who also spent a good deal of time writing articles in which his own work and that of Auden, Spender, and MacNeice was clearly identified as the Poetry of the Day, contributed a 'Letter to a Young Revolutionary' to *New Country*. In this letter he earnestly advised his undergraduate friend 'to divide your outrageously long holidays between three activities'. These he listed as,

1. Investigating the temper of the people . . .
2. Investigating the methods of capitalism . . .
3. Promoting the will to obey.

This last injunction is carefully glossed; it means that the young man must learn to submit 'to his natural leader'. This almost Messianic notion of The Leader runs through the poetry of the period, as it does through the politics. The Leader was not, however, a solitary, but a man accompanied by a select band of other explorers and adventurers. This explains another of the characteristic notes sounded by the poetry of the time – that note of the hortatory and the evangelical which is also, simultaneously, chatty and cosy. One is reminded over and over again of the Labour Party spokesman talking to a vast audience of 'Our old friend Hughie', or 'Nye', or 'Ernie'. One is reminded also, and less comfortably, of the headmaster at speechday. A good deal of personality-bandying goes on. Charles Madge, in a couple of lines already noted by Julian Symons in his admirable evocation of the period, says in a *Letter to the Intelligentsia*

> But there waited for me in the summer morning
> Auden, fiercely. I read, shuddered and knew.

Auden is the main personality to be used in verse of this kind, but other names do crop up. Some observers at the time felt that to be 'named' in a poem was to be accepted as a member of the intellectual junta which saw itself as a kind of Revolutionary Council of the Intelligentsia. This was a not altogether fair criticism; the poets were much less certain of their political colours than some would have us believe. For one thing, a poet with a *bourgeois* upbringing could not easily speak as a member of the working class. Consequently, he must see himself as the divided creature he is and speak out of the conflict between his environment and his convictions. This sounds well, but leaves the main question unanswered. Is the writer primarily concerned to produce propaganda, or is his first concern the creation of works of high aesthetic merit? It is no use denying that the most efficient propaganda is likely to be of a low intellectual content. On the other hand, to indulge in profound intellectual subtleties is, perhaps, to absent oneself from the Great Struggle, and thus to betray those very values by which one is so concerned to live.

These arguments were very much to the fore in the early thirties. C. Day Lewis in *Revolution in Writing* (1935) after having shown a tendency to place his trust in Marx first and the Muse second, by publishing much propagandist verse, came to the most generally acceptable conclusion. 'A good poem . . . enters deep into the stronghold of our emotions: if it is written by a good revolutionary, it is bound to have a revolutionary effect on our emotions, and therefore to be essentially – though not formally – propaganda.' This conclusion looks very much like a compromise arranged in order to give the poet both the comfort of belonging to a 'movement' and the freedom to ignore its dogmas; it is one with the numerous attempts to prove that communism was the true heir to the liberal tradition, the most sensitive exponent of this belief being Stephen Spender in his *Forward From Liberalism* (1937). He announced that 'the World State will not be the standardized world which the imperialists and fascists fear, or say they fear. The aim of communism is, as Lenin wrote, to create multiformity.' He, like many others, saw the true communist society as one in which every individual could truly realize himself. This may now seem a rather odd belief, but we must do the Spender of those days the justice to reflect that if communism has not provided this ideal situation, neither has liberal democracy.

Spender's concern with the fate of the lonely individual spirit was shared by many people. Although some, if not all, left-wing writers were able to accept Soviet purges, as tending to the good of the greatest number and, therefore, ultimately to the good of the individual; and though there was much talk of 'mass movements' and 'class', the liberal's concern for the solitary human being was at the heart of the thirties crusading zeal. I use the word 'crusading' deliberately, for there was something religious in the moral fervour of the time. The poets had, in their own eyes, taken on the role of preachers. This, of course, made it essential that they should, in all respects, conform to the doctrine which they put forward, and one aspect of the 'cosiness' I have mentioned, is the way in which individuals are taken to task by their colleagues for showing a less than saint-like integrity. *New Verse* (always a little suspicious of the spiritual purity of political zealots) devoted a page and a half to the downfall of C. Day Lewis when he became one of the selectors for The Book Society. Geoffrey Grigson commented:

The Book Society is a Limited Company pimping to the mass *bourgeois* mind and employing 'distinguished' members of the literary underworld, *adopters* of literature as a profession, writers each of no more real existence than a tick lost in the last five minutes of a cuckoo clock. On this Committee, Mr Day Lewis no doubt will be Change, Revolution, Youth, the Rising Generation. But this ends his stance as the Poet writing thrillers (result: respectful, knowing reviews of each thriller) and establishes him as the Thriller Writer, the Underworld Man, the yesterday's newspaper, the grease in the sink-pipe of letters who has been posed for ten years as spring water.

Think of Hardy, Yeats, Housman, Flecker, Pound, Lawrence, Eliot, Graves, Auden, Spender, Madge – could one have gone so treasonably against what is real? Mr Day Lewis and his Legend are now liquidated: the liquid has flowed to its oily shape and low level in the old sardine tin of Respectability. Mr Lewis has drained himself off, a Noyes, a Binyon, a Squire, a dullard.

We can get along without him.

This illustrates perfectly the way in which many thirties people regarded poets as heroes who must be of spotless virtue if they were not to sully the cause for which they fought. *New Verse* was as watchful for errors as a heresy-hunting inquisitor. It commented sourly and sadly upon Auden's acceptance of the King's Medal. It commented derisively on Pound's, Eliot's and Herbert Read's attraction to Social Credit. In passing, it dismissed Middleton Murry as an 'unbalanced mythomaniac monster', and referred to Edmund Blunden as 'The Merton Field-mouse'. It reserved most of its fury, however, for those writers who had chosen to worship other and false gods, or who had, after an early adherence to the faith, lapsed from grace.

This may sound as if the 'faith' was definable; it wasn't. Offences against it were, however, easy to perceive, and not always difficult to deride. One of the things which made *New Verse*, edited by Geoffrey Grigson, at first alone and then with the help of Kenneth Allott, so emphatically *the* magazine of the period was its radical distrust of anything worn out, evasive, shoddy, or meretricious, and its gay pillorying of those it felt to be pedlars of any kind of *kitsch*. Though Grigson had his favourite targets (he found it difficult to see or say anything good about Michael Roberts, or Edmund Blunden, or Edith Sitwell), he and his magazine were, on the whole, remarkably objective in their chastisements, and the respect in which the magazine was held is shown by the way in which a poet who had been ridiculed in one issue would allow his poems to be published in the next. Even those poets in whose interests the magazine might be said to have been founded were liable to get their wrists slapped on occasion. Neither MacNeice nor Auden escaped whipping, and George Barker once received a review headed simply 'Nertz'. This heading shows how the distrust of the pretentious and the sham could lead *New Verse* into trivial snook-cocking, but this was, perhaps, a healthier error of taste than that which led so many other periodicals into dull sententiousness. Moreover, behind the jokes there was often, one feels, real shame, real anger, as perhaps in:

FAN MAIL FOR A POET

To be read over a network of high-power Radio Stations by an American Hot-gospeller.

HOW NICE for a man to be clever,
So famous, so true;
So sound an investment; how EVER
So nice to be YOU.

To peer into basements, up alleys,
A nose for the search.
To challenge with pertinent sallies,
And then JOIN the Church.

First comes Prufrock, then Sweeney, and then
Thomas à Becket.
How frightfully nice of the good men
In cloth to forget it.

The broad-backed Hippo so weak and frail
Succumbed to the shock.
But the TRUE Church now can never fail,
Based upon 'THE ROCK'.

As a POET you visit today
The NICE Portuguese.
You can help England so in this way;
I DO hope you please.

You WILL watch Spain's terrible border;
Take care where you tread.
How AWFUL for England if you were
Shot down for a 'RED'.

I like you, and what's more I READ you:
There are such a few
Christian Poets so noble; indeed you
Must know it – YOU DO.

How nice for a man to be clever
So famous, so true;
So sound an investment; how EVER
So nice to be YOU.

W. T. NETTLEFOLD

This poem is a lament for a lost leader. Eliot had betrayed the admiration and respect shown him by the thirties men, not only by turning to orthodox religion after his mockery of it, but also by visiting a fascist country which was helping Franco in the Spanish Civil War. This again illustrates the way in which a poet was regarded as a person whose actions were as publicly important as his poems.

If the thirties men remind us of schoolboys in their mythologizing and in their ragging, they may also remind us of a schoolboy's passionate sense of honour. Poets who 'suck up' to the Establishment, reviewers who pander to *bourgeois* tastes, together with all prigs, plagiarists, pedants, and bores, are an offence and should be publicly pilloried. They have offended against the unspoken code of decency which is, in different ways, the theology of all public school products. Nor are they interesting or lively enough to be regarded as eccentrics, and therefore acceptable. They have actually *chosen* to be beyond the pale, sometimes for profit, but sometimes, more dreadfully, because they actually *like* it.

Much of the *New Verse* attitude over these matters can be seen in the affair of Geoffrey Grigson and 'the old Jane'. In 1934 Edith Sitwell's *Aspects of Modern Poetry* was reviewed by G. W. Stonier in the *New Statesman*. He found marked resemblances between this book and F. R. Leavis's *New Bearings in English Poetry*, which had been published for some time, and considered this odd as Miss Sitwell was at some pains in her book to show her opposition to Leavis's viewpoint. Not long afterwards Geoffrey Grigson discovered several parallels between Herbert Read's essay on Hopkins and Miss Sitwell's. Bonamy Dobrée in the *Listener* also made similar discoveries. In *New Verse* 12 Grigson wrote a scathing attack on the Sitwell family, 'these three versifying odd-medods', and in spite of a final recommendation ('best leave these minimal creatures, these contemptible elvers, wriggling away in their dull habitat') delightedly printed in several succeeding issues quotations from Miss Sitwell's various contributions to the Press, giving them satirical headlines and attributing them to 'the old Jane'. It seems almost as if Sitwell-baiting was a necessary ritual for the thirties men. *Twentieth Century Verse*, edited by Julian Symons, printed the following astonishing item in its tenth issue:

NOTE ON EMINENCE

The New Coterie (No. 1, Nov. 1935) printed this letter, in reply to a circular sent out to a number of writers and artists, asking them to send work:

Sir,

I am requested by Miss Edith Sitwell to return the enclosed communication, which was doubtless sent to her by mistake. Writers of Miss Sitwell's standing do not 'submit' their works for approval. . . . Miss Sitwell asks me to assure you that she does not suspect you of deliberate bad manners; your mistake is possibly the result of lack of experience in dealing with writers of eminence.

Yours faithfully,
M. Grogan
(for Miss Sitwell)

This is much too good to be lost.

There would be no point in spending so much time upon the attention paid by the thirties men to this particular poet, if it were not that, in a curious way, she became a symbol of much that they most detested. Aristocratic by birth and by assertion, she could not fail to rile the left-wingers. Inclined to regard emotive phrase-spinning as literary criticism, and to accept her private intuitions in matters of literary value as authoritative, she could not but infuriate writers who had sat at the feet of I. A. Richards, and who valued precision of thought in critical analysis. Moreover, and perhaps even more irritatingly, Miss Sitwell presented to the public an image of the poet which was far more effective theatrically than anything a thirties man could dare to invent, and also opposed in every way to that image of the poet in society which the thirties generation was busy trying to clarify. Even the notion of the intellectual *élite* which was to lead the mass movement towards the New World Socialist State was in direct contrast with the Sitwellian Threesome, an *élite* of altogether another and gaudier variety. One might even say that the Sitwells provided the thirties men with an invaluable point of reference; moreover, Geoffrey Grigson's references to 'the old Jane' probably did as much to increase the circulation of *New Verse* as anything else – a debt which he acknowledged in his first book of poems, *Several*

Observations, by following the dedication, 'To Bertschy', with another, reading,

> And on second thoughts,
> also for my publicity manager,
> *Edith Sitwell*,
> with love and thanks.

Behind all the jokes there lay a serious purpose, however. The question of the poet's image was very important to the men of the thirties. It almost seems as if the main task of many poets was to make an assertion about the poet's function, rather than to perform that function. Some of the propagandist poems convince us more of the writer's belief in the importance of writing propaganda than of his emotional commitment to his statements. Frequently the image of the poet gets in the way of the poetry. The new-style laurel wreath is worn self-consciously, and with the fashionable tilt to the left. It is, however, difficult to keep on, when you're not used to it, so the conversation often becomes stilted. While the thirties men had all the advantages of sharing (generally speaking) a social credo, they had also to suffer the disadvantages of being members of a group which demanded that they play a particular role. This role could, however, be interpreted in several ways, and as the thirties progressed some poets took the general belief in the importance of individual fulfilment to its logical extreme, and became involved in the use of dream-language, automatic writing, and all the paraphernalia of Surrealism. Nothing could be more opposed, one would imagine, to the tenets of the left-wing poets who made up the *avant-garde* of the first years of the decade, and yet it seems that when, in 1935, the younger poets began to produce this irrational, nightmarish, outrageously introverted poetry, the Old Guard were far from dismayed.

A part of the reason for this must be laid at the door of Freud. To some revolutionaries it seemed that, though

Marx was God, Freud was his Prophet. Both had icono-
clastic effects; both upset the *bourgeoisie* and laid bare the
springs of action. Both explained personal and social
motivation in a new way. 'When Sigmund Freud called
man's attention to his unconscious,' wrote C. Day Lewis,
'he set moving a process the results of which may well
prove as important as those of the Industrial Revolution or
the discovery of America . . . Freud, because of the enor-
mous emphasis he lays on the individual, is the real cham-
pion of liberalism today.' Auden, in his 'In Memory
of Sigmund Freud' published in *Another Time* (1940),
wrote:

> No wonder the ancient cultures of conceit
> In his technique of unsettlement foresaw
> The fall of princes, the collapse of
> Their lucrative patterns of frustration. . .

Freud, then, was somehow a republican and a socialist,
toppling the princes and undermining the capitalists. Thus
any Freudian *exposé* of the way we are is a Revolutionary
document.

Such was a fairly widely held attitude towards Freud, and
towards the surrealistic, or near-surrealistic poetry that
began to appear in the middle of the decade from David
Gascoyne, Hugh Sykes Davies, Philip O'Connor, and
others. Day Lewis, who saw Freudian Liberalism and the
Mass Revolutionary Movement as ultimately opposed to
one another, though temporarily allied in the struggle to
overcome the Bad Old System, wrote in a postscript of 1936
to his *A Hope for Poetry* (1934), of a 'new generation of
poets' that was 'not so much influenced by the "New
Country" school as reacting away from it.' He listed the
poets as 'George Barker, Dylan Thomas, Clifford Dyment,
David Gascoyne.' Certainly these poets (and one could
add the names of Ruthven Todd, Roy Fuller, Bernard
Spencer, and Kenneth Allott), do not have quite the same

mannerisms as their elders. They tend to be less straight-forwardly didactic. When wishing to state a lesson, they use the form of the fable. Sometimes they seem to be simply exploiting a taste for the grotesque. These differences from the 'New Countrymen' are, however, less basic than they appeared in 1936. For one thing, all the characteristics I have mentioned can be found in Auden and in MacNeice even before 1936. The important difference between the early and the late thirties men is less a difference of technique, than a difference of emphasis. The image of the poet provided by most of the contributors to *Contemporary Poetry and Prose* differs from that provided by *New Verses* from 1933 to 1936, in being more obviously 'romantic'. The poet is still a teacher, but a wielder of symbols rather than a commentator. Moreover, the attitude towards the social situation is more savagely despairing, more brutally mocking. The note of urbanity is replaced by a form of controlled hysteria; the ordered delineation of a disintegrating society is replaced by a deliberate distortion, expressive, rather than descriptive, of social and moral disorder. The poet presented by the extremists among the young in 1935 is the victim rather than the leader of society. One problem faced by his elders has been solved; he does not write as a *bourgeois* pretending to be a member of the working class, but out of his own disintegration as a sample *bourgeois*. This is the logical Marxist answer. The *bourgeois* cannot change his spots; let his diseases be spotlit.

Neat though this analysis may be, it is not really a fair one. The new generation were not, in general, extremists. Many writers, like Kenneth Allott and David Gascoyne, could write in a 'New Country' manner as well as in a surrealist one, and surrealism made its contribution more in terms of translations than in original English poems. George Reavey, David Gascoyne, Humphrey Jennings, A. L. Lloyd, and others translated a great deal of the work of the French surrealists. Collections by both Benjamin Peret and

Paul Éluard were published. David Gascoyne wrote *A Short Survey of Surrealism* (1935). The Surrealist Exhibition of 1936 was visited by over 20,000 people and widely discussed. Surrealism, however, remained very much a continental affair. It provided the thirties men with some fresh techniques. A few outright surrealist poems were achieved. On the whole, it must be regarded as an influential idea rather than as another movement in the history of twentieth-century English poetry – at least, so far. It is from a surrealist, however, that one of the central statements of the period comes. André Breton said, 'Let it be clearly understood that for us, Surrealists, the interests of thought cannot cease to go hand in hand with the interests of the working class and all armed attacks on it cannot fail to be considered by us as attacks on thought likewise.' Here the propagandist and the poet, the mass observer and the introvert, are all (apart from the word surrealists) in agreement; this is the central dogma of the thirties' generation of writers.

It is not inappropriate that such a statement should be made by a surrealist believing in 'the omnipotence of the dream', for the thirties are dream-ridden. Mere social commentary is not the heart of the poets' attitude, though a sociological credo may be at the heart of the expressed convictions of the period. The blurred borderlands between real and unreal, boyhood and manhood, game and ritual, vision and fantasy, fable and history, are the territories in which the poets of the thirties live, and no one more than Auden.

We come back, then, finally, to Auden. He is the clear Master of the Period. He dominates it from first to last. His sovereignty is never seriously in doubt, though, from the vantage point of 1963, many of those early poems appear less accomplished than some by his contemporaries. The satirical note is often shrill, and there is often a schoolboy knowingness, an eager relishing of the audience's probable shocked response. And yet these aspects are all subordinate to Auden's main virtue, which was his assumption that poetry did actually *have* an audience, and that poetry *could* be changed into a valuable instrument of social health. This is a point of view taken up by Dylan Thomas in the Auden double number of *New Verse* which was published in November 1937 when Auden was thirty. This tribute to Auden includes a check-list of all his writings, a reproduction of one of his manuscripts, his poem 'Dover' and reminiscences of him and essays on his work from Christopher Isherwood, Stephen Spender, Louis MacNeice, Geoffrey Grigson, Kenneth Allott, and Edgell Rickword. These essays are followed by a series of shorter comments. Dylan Thomas's is acute.

I sometimes think of Mr Auden's poetry as a hygiene, a knowledge and practice, based on a brilliantly prejudiced analysis of contemporary disorders, relating to the preservation and promotion of health, a sanitary science and a flusher of melancholies. I sometimes think of his poetry as a great war, admire intensely the mature, religious, and logical fighter, and deprecate the boy bushranger.

I think he is a wide and deep poet, and that his first narrow angles, of pedantry and careful obscurity, are worn almost all away. I think he is as technically sufficient, and as potentially productive of greatness, as any poet writing in English. He makes Mr Yeats's isolation guilty as a trance.

P.S. – Congratulations on Auden's seventieth birthday.

The postscript is, perhaps, a necessary reminder of the age at which Auden achieved this extraordinary position among his contemporaries. Other comments are as illuminating of the period as of the regard in which Auden was held. Berthold Viertel regards him as essentially a schoolmaster, though one with Swiftian qualities. He says that, 'He is apt to indulge in a cosmic humour which is sometimes sidetracked into sheer joking – even into a kind of practical joking – reminding us that the school-teacher still harbours traces of the schoolboy.' Allen Tate confesses to not rating

Auden as highly as *New Verse* does, and detects in Spender and Auden 'a juvenile and provincial point of view'. On the other hand, Auden and MacNeice are 'tough minds and real poets'. George Barker finds Auden's poetry exhilarating but discerns 'a clumsy interrogatory finger questioning me about my matriculation certificate, my antecedents, and my annual income'. He also senses 'a sort of general conspiratorial wink being made behind my back to a young man who sometimes has the name Christopher, sometimes Stephen, sometimes Derek, and sometimes Wystan'. He dislikes its 'snobbery of clique'.

The longer essays are as perceptive, and as objective as the majority of the comments. What emerges, indeed, is not a paean of praise, but a vote of confidence. Almost every supporter has some criticism to make. Though words like 'genius' are used, they are used with much wagging of warning fingers. The total picture is of a poet whose dominance is inescapable, partly because he is clearly a leader, an innovator, but also very largely because he is representative of his time, and of his generation. Day Lewis, despite the previous month's comments upon his Book Society activities, is allowed to make the point:

His satire has been criticized at times as irresponsible: this is to misunderstand its motive and aim: in so far as it proceeds from the life of one social class, a class which has lost its responsibility and civilizing impetus, the terms of this satire are bound to be superficially irresponsible. But no contemporary writing shows so clearly the revulsion of the artist from a society which can no longer support him, his need to identify himself with a class that can provide for his imagination.

Edgell Rickword, in a brief article on 'Auden and Politics', is less kind, seeing Auden's work as an expression of 'the feeling of insecurity that afflicts a section of the middle classes as the ceaseless concentration of capital into fewer hands undermines their comparatively privileged position'. He suggests that Auden's first collection showed 'the impact of after-the-war reality in a certain environment on the dream-world of the growing boy'.

As one reads the periodicals of the time it sometimes seems as if the whole of the thirties generation was engaged in analysing its predicament and writing poetry and criticism about it, and was left-wing to a man (though election results show that it was not). Although the mass-movement it so earnestly envisaged did not, in fact, occur, it did itself constitute a kind of mass movement. It was not a purely socialist movement; nor was it even a social one: I can only describe it as a movement of the passionate conscience. Each poem was an exploration for health, and many were only superficially concerned with political realities. Many poems are searches for new rituals, new games, new disciplines, and use the terminology of social criticism for this purpose. The terror that lurks around the corner in some of Auden's poems may be couched in terms of Europe, but it communicates as a personal nightmare. Some poems, at once explicitly sociological and deeply personal, invoke nature as a restorer, not of repose, but of strength and fecundity. What gives the best of the period's poetry its unmistakable quality seems to be the way in which feelings of private and of communal insecurity are fused together, so that the personal lyrical anguish informs the political statement.

The poets of the time were fully aware of this aspect of the situation, as Day Lewis's and Edgell Rickword's comments have shown. They knew that much of their political activity was born of private necessity rather than public conviction. And yet, reading all the manifestoes and symposia, all the letters and analyses and critiques, it seems as if these poets really did believe that a poet could be an effective modern prophet. They talked in an almost empty theatre as if it were a packed Wembley Stadium. They argued, proved, disproved, and judged, as if the whole nation were listening. They had, in fact, discovered a drama and invented an audience. This, of all the thirties phenomena is perhaps the most fascinating. These poems of social criticism were almost all aimed at people who did not exist, at least in the roles assumed by the poems. Their assurance and poise is a pretence. Their prophecies are made to a handful of the converted.

Of course, some few books of poems did achieve a wide circulation during this period, and the Left Book Club had a large audience for its discussions and arguments, but it was in the forties that the poets of the thirties found their widest public, and it may be that it is in the sixties, now the dust has settled, that the achievement of that poetic generation in that crucial decade may come to be properly evaluated. I wonder, indeed, whether these poems did not help to turn men's minds towards the creation of a welfare state after the war. Have they any responsibility for the new wave of social comment in the novel and in poetry at present? These are unanswerable questions, but it is time to ask them, and to make some attempt to understand and appreciate the work of that period of unease, threatened by war as we are threatened, troubled by social and racial conflicts as we are troubled, and to wonder whether or not an anthology of this kind is a piece of literary history, or an illumination of our own present discomforts.

Victoria B.C.
June 1964   ROBIN SKELTON

A Note on the Texts Used

In order to allow each poem to be seen in its correct position in the period, I have dated each one. The letter 'p' before a date means that the poem was first printed in a periodical or anthology of that year; the letter 'c' means that the poem was published in a collection of work by the poet concerned at that time; the letter 'w' shows that the date given is the date of composition. Where the poets themselves have attached dates to their poems I have not added any other details. I would have preferred to place the dates of composition, first printing, and first collection, all beside each poem; this has, however, proved quite impossible, so my date must be regarded simply as a rough guide to the place of the poem in the decade, rather than as a precise statement of the time of origin. In some cases, of course, the poems appeared first in collections, and never appeared in periodicals at all. In the absence of a complete bibliography of all the poets involved it is impossible to get the situation as clear as one would ideally wish. It will, however, be noticed that the great majority of these poems first appeared or were first collected between 1936 and 1940, and that relatively few appeared first in the years 1930–5. This is not the result of carelessness. In fact, most of the poems we think of as thirties poems were produced in the second half of the decade. As Julian Symons has pointed out, the years 1936–7 were the very heart of the thirties experience. Common sense also indicates that as the decade proceeded more of our young poets began to publish their work, and the work of their elders improved.

Many poets revise their work considerably after its first appearance in a periodical. I have, in this anthology, tended to use early rather than late texts, assuming the earlier ones to be more significant from the period point of view. Thus the texts are always those of the dates given, and not those of a later period. This is not an important matter for most of the poets represented here, but it is important for some; W. H. Auden, in particular, has altered his early verse almost out of recognition.

In titling these poems I have in almost all cases used the titles given at the date to which the poems are ascribed. The only exceptions are Dylan Thomas, where I have preferred to use the style made familiar to us by his *Collected Poems*, and Roy Fuller, whose 'Centaurs' and 'End of a City' were originally untitled. In the case of Auden I have compromised. As it was a much admired feature of his *Poems* (1930) that the poems had numbers, not titles, I have kept the numbers for the poems which were first collected in that book. For later poems I have adopted the conventional device of using the first line where a title was not provided by Auden. All other poems have the titles originally given them at their first appearances in periodical or book.

I should also explain that where an author has shared a volume with one or two others I have regarded this publication as a collection of the poet's own, rather than as an anthology. Thus those poems by Ruthven Todd, H. B. Mallalieu, and Peter Hewitt which appeared in *Poets of Tomorrow*, 1 (1939) are dated 'c. 1939', and the poems of Edgar Foxall from *Proems* (1938) are similarly dated.

*

In the preparation of this work I must first of all thank Kenneth Allott, Geoffrey Grigson, and Julian Symons, all of whom played such important parts in the thirties, for answering my queries, and lending me material, and making many valuable suggestions. Without their assistance my task would have been impossible to complete. I must also express my gratitude for the loan of material to Michael Holroyd, John Knight, John Jump, Ruth Jump, and Tony Connor.

The generosity of Charles Sewter in giving me copies of several periodicals of the time has also placed me under a heavy load of obligation. It is to the poets themselves, however, that my thanks must be expressed the most forcibly. They have not only allowed me to reprint their work, but have, in many cases, allowed me to reprint work of which they no longer approve, or early unrevised versions of poems they have reshaped. I cannot over-emphasize my gratitude to them for this. W. H. Auden has been monumentally generous in allowing me to use early texts of five poems of which he now disapproves. These poems are 'Sir, No Man's Enemy', 'A Communist to Others', 'To a Writer on his Birthday', 'Spain', and 'September 1, 1939'. I have agreed to make it absolutely clear that 'Mr W. H. Auden considers these five poems to be trash which he is ashamed to have written'. I am most grateful to Mr Auden for putting the needs of this anthology before his own personal wishes in this manner.

I am similarly grateful to Roy Fuller for allowing me to print an early version of 'End of a City' rather than the version in his *Collected Poems*. I would also like to thank David Gascoyne for allowing me to use poems he has discarded from his forthcoming collected volume, and for giving me much useful information. Philip O'Connor also drew my attention to work I might otherwise have missed seeing, as did Bernard Spencer and Gavin Ewart. Although I cannot list any but one or two of the books I have used in exploring the period, I would like to make special mention of Julian Symon's fascinating book *The Thirties* (Cresset, 1960) which, together with Robert Graves's and Alan Hodge's *The Long Weekend* (Faber 1941) and James Laver's scrapbook, *Between the Wars* (Vista, 1961), may appeal to readers of this Anthology as giving a more detailed picture of the period than I have been able to do in my Introduction.

R.S.

I. IN OUR TIME

III

August is nearly over, the people
  Back from holiday are tanned
With blistered thumbs and a wallet of snaps and a little
  Joie de vivre which is contraband;
Whose stamina is enough to face the annual
  Wait for the annual spree,
Whose memories are stamped with specks of sunshine
  Like faded *fleurs-de-lys*.
Now the till and the typewriter call the fingers,
  The workman gathers his tools
For the eight-hour day but after that the solace
  Of films or football pools
Or of the gossip or cuddle, the moments of self-glory
  Or self-indulgence, blinkers on the eyes of doubt,
The blue smoke rising and the brown lace sinking
  In the empty glass of stout.
Most are accepters, born and bred to harness,
  And take things as they come,
But some refusing harness and more who are refused it
  Would pray that another and a better Kingdom come,
Which now is sketched in the air or travestied in slogans
  Written in chalk or tar on stucco or plaster-board
But in time may find its body in men's bodies,
  Its law and order in their heart's accord,
Where skill will no longer languish nor energy be tram-
    melled
  To competition and graft,
Exploited in subservience but not allegiance
  To an utterly lost and daft

System that gives a few at fancy prices
　　Their fancy lives
While ninety-nine in the hundred who never attend the
　　　banquet
　　Must wash the grease of ages off the knives.
And now the tempter whispers 'But you also
　　Have the slave-owner's mind,
Would like to sleep on a mattress of easy profits,
　　To snap your fingers or a whip and find
Servants or houris ready to wince and flatter
　　And build with their degradation your self-esteem;
What you want is not a world of the free in function
　　But a niche at the top, the skimmings of the cream.'
And I answer that that is largely so for habit makes me
　　Think victory for one implies another's defeat,
That freedom means the power to order, and that in order
　　To preserve the values dear to the élite
The élite must remain a few. It is so hard to imagine
　　A world where the many would have their chance without
A fall in the standard of intellectual living
　　And nothing left that the highbrow cared about.
Which fears must be suppressed. There is no reason for
　　　thinking
　　That, if you give a chance to people to think or live,
The arts of thought or life will suffer and become rougher
　　And not return more than you could ever give.
And now I relapse to sleep, to dreams perhaps and reaction
　　Where I shall play the gangster or the sheikh,
Kill for the love of killing, make the world my sofa,
　　Unzip the women and insult the meek.
Which fantasies no doubt are due to my private history,
　　Matter for the analyst,
But the final cure is not in his past-dissecting fingers
　　But in a future of action, the will and fist
Of those who abjure the luxury of self-pity
　　And prefer to risk a movement without being sure

If movement would be better or worse in a hundred
  Years or a thousand when their heart is pure.
None of our hearts are pure, we always have mixed motives,
  Are self-deceivers, but the worst of all
Deceits is to murmur 'Lord, I am not worthy'
  And, lying easy, turn your face to the wall.
But may I cure that habit, look up and outwards
  And may my feet follow my wider glance
First no doubt to stumble, then to walk with the others
  And in the end – with time and luck – to dance.

c. 1939   LOUIS MACNEICE

Song for the New Year

It's farewell to the drawing-room's civilised cry
The professor's sensible whereto and why
The frock-coated diplomat's social aplomb
Now matters are settled with gas and with bomb.

The works for two pianos, the brilliant stories
Of reasonable giants and remarkable fairies,
The pictures, the ointments, the fragile wares,
And the branches of olive are stored upstairs.

For the Devil has broken parole and arisen
He has dynamited his way out of prison
Out of the well where his Papa throws
The rebel angel, the outcast rose.

Like influenza he walks abroad,
He stands on the bridge, he waits by the ford;
As a goose or a gull he flies overhead,
He hides in the cupboards and under the bed.

Assuming such shapes as may best disguise
The hate that burns in his big blue eyes
He may be a baby that croons in its pram,
Or a dear old grannie boarding a tram;

A plumber, a doctor, for he has skill
To adopt a serious profession at will;
Superb at ice-hockey, a prince at the dance,
He's fierce as the tigers, secretive as plants.

O were he to triumph, dear heart, you know
To what depths of shame he would drag you low,
He would steal you away from me, yes, my dear,
He would steal you and cut off your marvellous hair.

Millions already have come to their harm,
Succumbing like doves to his adder's charm;
Hundreds of trees in the wood are unsound
I'm the axe that must cut them down to the ground.

For I, after all, am the fortunate one,
The Happy-go-Lucky, the spoilt third son;
For me it is written the Devil to chase,
And to rid the earth of the human race.

The behaving of man is a world of horror,
A sedentary Sodom and slick Gomorrah
I must take charge of the liquid fire
And storm the cities of human desire;

The buying, and selling, the eating and drinking,
The disloyal machines and irreverent thinking,
The lovely dullards again and again
Inspiring their bitter ambitious men.

I shall come, I shall punish, the Devil be dead,
I shall have caviare thick on my bread
I shall build myself a cathedral for home,
With a vacuum cleaner in every room.

I shall ride on the front in a platinum car,
My features shall shine, my name shall be star:
Day long and night long the bells I shall peal
And down the long street I shall turn the cart wheel.

So Little John, Long John, Polly and Peg,
And poor little Horace with only one leg,
You must leave your breakfast, your desk, and your play
On a fine summer morning the Devil to slay.

For it's order and trumpet and anger and drum,
And power and glory command you to come:
The graves shall fly open and suck you all in
And the earth shall be emptied of mortal sin.

The fishes are silent deep in the sea,
The skies are lit up like a Christmas tree
The star in the West shoots its warning cry
'Mankind is alive, but mankind must die'.

So good-bye to the house with its wallpaper red,
Good-bye to the sheets on the warm double bed,
Good-bye to the beautiful birds on the wall,
It's good-bye, dear heart, good-bye to you all.

p. 1937   W. H. AUDEN

The Magnetic Mountain

32

You that love England, who have an ear for her music,
The slow movement of clouds in benediction,
Clear arias of light thrilling over her uplands,
Over the chords of summer sustained peacefully;

Ceaseless the leaves' counterpoint in a west wind lively,
Blossom and river rippling loveliest allegro,
And the storms of wood strings brass at year's finale:
Listen. Can you not hear the entrance of a new theme?

You who go out alone, on tandem or on pillion,
Down arterial roads riding in April,
Or sad beside lakes where hill-slopes are reflected
Making fires of leaves, your high hopes fallen:
Cyclists and hikers in company, day excursionists,
Refugees from cursed towns and devastated areas:
Know you seek a new world, a saviour to establish
Long-lost kinship and restore the blood's fulfilment.

You who like peace, good sorts, happy in a small way
Watching birds or playing cricket with schoolboys,
Who pay for drinks all round, whom disaster chose not;
Yet passing derelict mills and barns roof-rent
Where despair has burnt itself out – hearts at a standstill,
Who suffer loss, aware of lowered vitality;
We can tell you a secret, offer a tonic; only
Submit to the visiting angel, the strange new healer.

You above all who have come to the far end, victims
Of a run-down machine, who can bear it no longer;
Whether in easy chairs chafing at impotence
Or against hunger, bullies and spies preserving
The nerve for action, the spark of indignation –
Need fight in the dark no more, you know your enemies.
You shall be leaders when zero hour is signalled,
Wielders of power and welders of a new world.

p. 1933   C. DAY LEWIS

An Elementary School Class Room in a Slum

Far far from gusty waves, these children's faces.
Like rootless weeds the torn hair round their paleness.
The tall girl with her weighed-down head. The paper-
Seeming boy with rat's eyes. The stunted unlucky heir
Of twisted bones, reciting a father's gnarled disease,
His lesson from his desk. At back of the dim class,
One unnoted, sweet and young: His eyes live in a dream
Of squirrels' game, in tree room, other than this.

On sour cream walls, donations. Shakespeare's head
Cloudless at dawn, civilized dome riding all cities.
Belled, flowery, Tyrolese valley. Open-handed map
Awarding the world its world. And yet, for these
Children, these windows, not this world, are world,
Where all their future's painted with a fog,
A narrow street sealed in with a lead sky,
Far far from rivers, capes, and stars of words.

Surely Shakespeare is wicked, the map a bad example
With ships and sun and love tempting them to steal –
For lives that slyly turn in their cramped holes
From fog to endless night? On their slag heap, these children
Wear skins peeped through by bones and spectacles of steel
With mended glass, like bottle bits on stones.
All of their time and space are foggy slum
So blot their maps with slums as big as doom.

Unless, governor, teacher, inspector, visitor,
This map becomes their window and these windows
That open on their lives like crouching tombs
Break, O break open, till they break the town

And show the children to the fields and all their world
Azure on their sands, to let their tongues
Run naked into books, the white and green leaves open
The history theirs whose language is the sun.

c. 1939   STEPHEN SPENDER

The Children

The young imagine their future in primary colours,
One climax inside another like Chinese boxes:
The military rescue *con brio*, or bearded explorer
Recording the flora of the Amazon;
Adventures improbable as Hans Andersen,
The gold where the rainbow is earthed round every street-
    corner,
The throttle wide open like delirium.

It is the sun ripens: heads bent over copybooks,
And the scratch of steel pens clutched and wielded inex-
    pertly
Lights the barbed wire between desire and performance,
Even when desire is stunted like the Arctic willow
And money and power and the fatal gifts of appearance
Whisper of the scope and freedom of the lavish sea.
Children stare through a metaphorical distance
Which conceals the psychotic, the cripple, and the refugee.

The earth-tremors grow infrequent and less violent
Coming to grips with the dimensional world.
Men stroll in the streets together less like a pageant,
The moon is not what is meant,
We lose the primitive energy of the word.
To the adolescent it appears again and again
Time is a gentleman with no time for him.

Men are exploded by necessity,
But let these children have no more to fear
Than denotes them human in a house of care.
Let them have flying poise like the stylized skater.
Love will send in his card at least for a time.
Let their hands be nimble as the hands of a juggler
Long after midnight to feel right as rain,
As free from responsibility as the insane.
The present and future shall fall together and kiss
Before the old teacher retire to his shrubs and pottering,
And the caretaker knock with his brush in the silent school-
　　room,
And the primers are locked away, and the class dismiss.

w. 1939　　　　　　　　　　　　　　KENNETH ALLOTT

In Our Time

Between the rough hills of gabbro and the cold sea,
Between the factory hooter and the snub-nosed bullet,
Folly grows up to its full height, but cannot grow for
　　ever.

Folly is built on pride, on pride and power,
And power ends in weariness and duty:
Even the hooded eagle cannot soar to heaven.

And the leader looks at last toward the people,
People asking for a home, a plot of earth,
A pageant in spring, and a sight of foreign merchants.

Power is built on fear and empty bellies:
Between the rough hills of gabbro and the cold sea
The gulls scream, squabbling for a poor harvest.

Between the factory hooter and the snub-nosed bullet,
Under the shadow of the guns, the corn ripens,
And folly cannot die, but cannot grow for ever.

c. 1939   MICHAEL ROBERTS

A Communist to Others

Comrades who when the sirens roar
From office shop and factory pour
           'Neath evening sky;
By cops directed to the fug
Of talkie-houses for a drug
Or down canals to find a hug
           Until you die:

We know, remember, what it is
That keeps you celebrating this
           Sad ceremonial;
We know the terrifying brink
From which in dreams you nightly shrink
'I shall be sacked without,' you think,
           'A testimonial.'

We cannot put on airs with you
The fears that hurt you hurt us too
           Only we say
That like all nightmares these are fake
If you would help us we could make
Our eyes to open, and awake
           Shall find night day.

On you our interests are set
Your sorrow we shall not forget
           While we consider

Those who in every country town
For centuries have done you brown,
But you shall see them tumble down
      Both horse and rider.

O splendid person, you who stand
In spotless flannels or with hand
      Expert on trigger;
Whose lovely hair and shapely limb
Year after year are kept in trim
Till buffers envy as you swim
      Your Grecian figure:

You're thinking us a nasty sight;
Yes, we are poisoned, you are right,
      Not even clean;
We do not know how to behave
We are not beautiful or brave
You would not pick our sort to save
      Your first fifteen.

You are not jealous yet, we know,
But we must warn you, even so
      So pray be seated:
It isn't cricket, but it's true
The lady who admires us, you
Have thought you're getting off with too,
      For you're conceited.

Your beauty's a completed thing.
The future kissed you, called you king,
      Did she? Deceiver!
She's not in love with you at all
No feat of yours can make her fall,
She will not answer to your call
      Like your retriever.

Dare-devil mystics who bear the scars
Of many spiritual wars
      And smoothly tell
The starving that their one salvation
Is personal regeneration
By fasting, prayer and contemplation;
        Is it? Well,

Others have tried it, all delight
Sustained in that ecstatic flight
      Could not console
When through exhausting hours they'd flown
From the alone to the Alone
Nothing remained but the dry-as-bone
      Night of the soul.

Coward; for all your goodness game
Your cream of Heaven is the same
      As any bounder's;
You hope to corner as reward
All that the rich can here afford
Love and music and bed and board
      While the world flounders.

And you, the wise man, full of humour
To whom our misery's a rumour
      And slightly funny;
Proud of your nicely balanced view
You say as if it were something new
The fuss we make is mostly due
      To lack of money.

Ah, what a little squirt is there
When of your aren't-I-charming air
      You stand denuded.
Behind your subtle sense of humour

You hide the boss's simple stuma
Among the foes which we enumer
          You are included.

Because you saw but were not indignant
The invasion of the great malignant
          Cambridge ulcer
That army intellectual
Of every kind of liberal
Smarmy with friendship but of all
          There are none falser.

A host of columbines and pathics
Who show the poor by mathematics
          In their defence
That wealth and poverty are merely
Mental pictures, so that clearly
Every tramp's a landlord really
          In mind-events.

The worst employer's double dealing
Is better than their mental-healing
          That would assist us.
The world, they tell us, has no flaws
Then is no need to change the laws
We're only not content because
          Jealous of sisters.

Once masters struck with whips; of recent
Years by being jolly decent
          For these are cuter
Fostering the heart's self-adulation
Would dissipate all irritation
Making a weakened generation
          Completely neuter.

Let fever sweat them till they tremble,
Cramp rack their limbs till they resemble
      Cartoons by Goya:
Their daughters sterile be in rut,
May cancer rot their herring gut,
The circular madness on them shut,
        Or paranoia.

Their splendid people, their wiseacres,
Professors, agents, magic-makers,
      Their poets and apostles,
Their bankers and their brokers too,
And Ironmasters shall turn blue
Shall fade away like morning dew
      With club-room fossils.

Unhappy poet, you whose only
Real emotion is feeling lonely
      When suns are setting;
Who fled in horror from all these
To islands in your private seas
Where thoughts like castaways find ease
      In endless petting:

You need us more than you suppose
And you could help us if you chose.
      In any case
We are not proud of being poor
In that of which you claim a store:
Return, be tender; or are we more
      Than you could face?

Comrades to whom our thoughts return,
Brothers for whom our bowels yearn
      When words are over;

Remember that in each direction
Love outside our own election
Holds us in unseen connection:
     O trust that ever.

p. 1933   W. H. AUDEN

Hymn

The splendid body is private, and calls for more.
No toy; not for a boy; but man to man, man to girl
runs blood, sweat oozes; each of us has a share.
All flesh is a flag and a secret code. Ring bells, then!
And throw away,
beginning from to-day
the eau-de-Cologne which disguised you, the stick which
  propped,
the tennis racquet, the blazer of the First Fifteen.
Don't kiss that dog, girl. Bachelor, your pipe is wood.
It is no good. Come away then. That must stop.
Some of you are still thinking what you might have been.
Don't do that, because it doesn't matter at all.

Come then, companions. This is the spring of blood,
heart's hey-day, movement of masses, beginning of good.

No more shall men take pride in paper and gold
in furs in cars in servants in spoons in knives.
But they shall love instead their friends and their wives,
owning their bodies at last, things which they have sold.
Come away then,
you fat man!
You don't want your watch-chain.
But don't interfere with us, because we know you too well.

If you do that you will lose your top hat
and be knocked on the head until you are dead.
Come with us, if you can, and, if not, go to hell
with your comfy chairs, your talk about the police,
your doll wife, your cowardly life, your newspaper, your
    interests in the East,
You, there, who are so patriotic, you liar, you beast!
Come, then, companions. This is the spring of blood,
heart's hey-day, movement of masses, beginning of good.

O poor young people! You, with the fidgeting hand,
who want to be understood, who want to understand,
now you must lie in the sun and walk erect and proud,
learn diving, learn to love, learn to hold a spade.
You who adore,
don't do it any more.
Give it right up,
and don't be a pup.
Isn't there anything on earth except your fidgeting hands?
Women won't help you, and it's a laugh to suppose they
    can;
and nor will stars; so if you can't get kissed,
don't bother to turn scientist and give yourself airs;
don't hide upstairs, but come out into the sun.

  Come then, companions. This is the spring of blood,
    heart's hey-day, movement of masses, beginning of good.

There is no need now to bribe and to take the bribe.
The king is flying, his regiments have melted like ice in
    spring.
Light has been let in. The fences are down. No broker is left
    alive.
There is no pretence about the singing in the streets and the
    dancing.

Come then, you who couldn't stick it,
  lovers of cricket, underpaid journalists,
  lovers of Nature, hikers, O touring cyclists,
now you must be men and women, and there is a chance.
Now you can join us, now all together sing All Power
not tomorrow but now in this hour, All Power
to lovers of life, to workers, to the hammer, the sickle, the
  blood.

Come then, companions. This is the spring of blood,
heart's hey-day, movement of masses, beginning of good.

p. 1933   REX WARNER

The Magnetic Mountain

25

Consider these, for we have condemned them;
Leaders to no sure land, guides their bearings lost
Or in league with robbers have reversed the signposts,
Disrespectful to ancestors, irresponsible to heirs.
Born barren, a freak growth, root in rubble,
Fruitlessly blossoming, whose foliage suffocates,
Their sap is sluggish, they reject the sun.

The man with his tongue in his cheek, the woman
With her heart in the wrong place, unhandsome, unwhole-
  some;
Have exposed the new-born to worse than weather,
Exiled the honest and sacked the seer.
These drowned the farms to form a pleasure-lake,
In time of drought they drain the reservoir
Through private pipes for baths and sprinklers.

Getters not begetters; gainers not beginners;
Whiners, no winners; no triers, betrayers;
Who steer by no star, whose moon means nothing.
Daily denying, unable to dig;
At bay in villas from blood relations,
Counters of spoons and content with cushions
They pray for peace, they hand down disaster.

They that take the bribe shall perish by the bribe,
Dying of dry rot, ending in asylums,
A curse to children, a charge on the state.
But still their fears and frenzies infect us;
Drug nor isolation will cure this cancer:
It is now or never, the hour of the knife,
The break with the past, the major operation.

c. 1933   C. DAY LEWIS

Nonsense

Sing a song of sixpence,
A pocketful of rye,
The lover's in the garden
The battle's in the sky.
The banker's in the city
Getting of his gold;
Oh isn't it a pity
The rye can't be sold.

The queen is drinking sherry
And dancing to a band;
A crowd may well feel merry
That it does not understand.

The banker turns his gold about
But that won't sell the rye,
Starve and grow cold without,
And ask the reason why
The guns are in the garden,
And battle's in the sky.

p. 1938   JULIAN BELL

The Magnetic Mountain

20

Fireman and farmer, father and flapper,
I'm speaking to you sir, please drop that paper;
Don't you know it's poison? Have you lost all hope?
Aren't you ashamed, ma'am, to be taking dope?
There's a nasty habit that starts in the head
And creeps through the veins till you go all dead:
Insured against accident? But that won't prove
Much use when one morning you find you can't move.

They tell you all's well with our lovely England
And God's in the capital. Isn't it grand
Where the offal of action, the rinsings of thought
From a stunted peer for a penny can be bought?
It seems a bargain, but in the long run
Will cost you your honour, your crops and your son.
They're selling you the dummy, for God's sake don't buy it!
Baby, that bottle's not clean, don't try it!

You remember that girl who turned the gas on? –
They drove her to it, they couldn't let her alone.
That young inventor – you all know his name –
They used the plans and he died of their fame.

63

Careful, climber, they're getting at your nerve!
Leader, that's a bribe, they'd like you to serve!
Bull, I don't want to give you a nightmare,
But – keep still a moment – are you quite sure you're there?

As for you, Bimbo, take off that false face!
You've ceased to be funny, you're in disgrace.
We can see the spy through that painted grin;
You may talk patriotic but you can't take us in.
You've poisoned the reservoirs, released your germs
On firesides, on foundries, on tubes and on farms.
You've made yourself cheap with your itch for power
Infecting all comers, a hopeless whore.

Scavenger barons and your jackal vassals,
Your pimping press-gang, your unclean vessels,
We'll make you swallow your words at a gulp
And turn you back to your element, pulp.
Don't bluster, Bimbo, it won't do you any good;
We can be much ruder and we're learning to shoot.
Closet Napoleon, you'd better abdicate,
You'd better quit the country before it's too late.

p. 1933   C. DAY LEWIS

Just a Smack at Auden

Waiting for the end, boys, waiting for the end.
What is there to be or do?
What's become of me or you?
Are we kind or are we true?
Sitting two and two, boys, waiting for the end.

Shall I build a tower, boys,
Knowing it will rend
Crack upon the hour, boys, waiting for the end?

Shall I pluck a flower, boys,
Shall I save or spend?
All turns sour, boys, waiting for the end.

Shall I send a wire, boys?
Where is there to send?
All are under fire, boys, waiting for the end.
Shall I turn a sire, boys?
Shall I choose a friend?
The fat is in the pyre, boys, waiting for the end.

Shall I make it clear, boys,
For all to apprehend,
Those that will not hear, boys, waiting for the end,
Knowing it is near, boys,
Trying to pretend,
Sitting in cold fear, boys, waiting for the end?

Look at all the wise, boys,
Can they stave or fend?
Can they keep from cries, boys, waiting for the end?
You can choose your ties, boys,
Whether pecked or henned.
All your wisdom dies, boys, waiting for the end.

Shall we send a cable, boys,
Accurately penned,
Knowing we are able, boys, waiting for the end,
Via the Tower of Babel, boys?
Christ will not ascend.
He's hiding in his stable, boys, waiting for the end.

Shall we blow a bubble, boys,
Glittering to distend,
Hiding from our trouble, boys, waiting for the end?
When you build on rubble, boys,
Nature will append
Double and redouble, boys, waiting for the end.

Shall we make a tale, boys,
That things are sure to mend,
Talking bluff and hale, boys, waiting for the end?
It will be born stale, boys,
Stinking to offend,
Dying ere it fail, boys, waiting for the end.

Shall we go all wild, boys,
Waste and make them lend,
Playing at the child, boys, waiting for the end?
It has all been filed, boys,
History has a trend,
Each of us enisled, boys, waiting for the end.

What was said by Marx, boys,
What did he perpend?
No good being sparks, boys, waiting for the end.
Treason of the clerks, boys,
Curtains that descend,
Lights becoming darks, boys, waiting for the end.

Waiting for the end, boys, waiting for the end.
Not a chance of blend, boys, things have got to tend.
Think of those who vend, boys, think of how we wend,
Waiting for the end, boys, waiting for the end.

p. 1937   WILLIAM EMPSON

A Note on Working-Class Solidarity

There will be no festivities when we lay down these tools,
For we are the massed grooves of grease-smooth systems.
The Communist measures the future, the Elect fear the past,
But we are those ribless polyps that nature insures
Against thought by routines, against triumph by tolerance,

66

Against life by the sense of mechanical footbeats,
Against protest by cant, extinction by syphilis,
And the glory of crucifixion by the price of timber.

p. 1933   EDGAR FOXALL

Audenesque for an Initiation

Don't forget the things we taught you by the broken water-
wheel,
Don't forget the middle classes fight much harder going
down hill,

Don't forget that new proscriptions are being posted now
and then,
Dr Johnson, Dr Leavis and the other Grand Old Men –

For, although they've often told us that they try to do their
best,
Are they up to the Full Fruit Standard, would they pass the
Spelling Test?

– Because we've got our eyes to keyholes, we know every-
thing they've done,
Lecturing on minor poets. 'Literature is quite good fun.'

And if you should try to fool us, imitate them, do the same,
We'll refuse your dummy bullets, we've had time to take
our aim.

We've been drinking stagnant water for some twenty years
or more
While the politicians slowly planned a bigger reservoir.

But we've dammed a different river, the water-wheel is
going again.
Now we've stopped designing sweaters and we've started in to
train.

We've given up the Georgian poets, teaching dance bands
  how to croon,
Bicycling in coloured goggles underneath a pallid moon.

We've destroyed the rotting signposts, made holes in all the
  pleasure-boats;
We'll pull down ancestral castles when we've time to swim
  the moats.

When we've practised we shall beat you with our Third or
  Fourth Fifteen,
In spite of Royalists on the touchline. 'Oh, well played,
  Sir!' 'Keep it clean!'

Our backs are fast as motor-cycles, all our forwards 20-
  stone.
Each of them can score unaided, running strongly on his own.

Every minute scouts give signals, come reporting what
  they've seen.
'Captain Ferguson is putting.' 'Undermine the 18th green.'

Before next month we'll storm the clubhouse. Messages are
  coming through:
'Darwin, doing cross-word puzzles, tries to find the missing
  clue.'

The *Times* Third Leaders are decoded, pigeon-holed for
  future use;
Tennyson has been convicted of incessant self-abuse.

We've been sending notes to Priestley, orange pips to Johnny
  Squire –
'Don't defend the trench you're holding.' 'Now the fat is in
  the fire.'

We've got control of all the railways and the perfume
  factories,
We're supercharged and have connection with the strongest
  batteries.

So if you feel like playing truant, remember that the game
  is up
Or you'll find that quite politely you've been sold a nasty
  pup.

p. 1933   GAVIN EWART

Newsreel

Enter the dream-house, brothers and sisters, leaving
Your debts asleep, your history at the door:
This is the home for heroes, and this loving
Darkness a fur you can afford.

Fish in their tank electrically heated
Nose without envy the glass wall: for them
Clerk, spy, nurse, killer, prince, the great and the defeated,
Move in a mute day-dream.

Bathed in this common source, you gape incurious
At what your active hours have willed –
Sleep-walking on that silver wall, the furious
Sick shapes and pregnant fancies of your world.

There is the mayor opening the oyster season:
A society wedding: the autumn hats look swell:
An old crocks' race, and a politician
In fishing-waders to prove that all is well.

Oh, look at the warplanes! Screaming hysteric treble
In the long power-dive, like gannets they fall steep.
But what are they to trouble –
These silver shadows to trouble your watery, womb-deep
  sleep?

See the big guns, rising, groping, erected
To plant death in your world's soft womb.
Fire-bud, smoke-blossom, iron seed projected –
Are these exotics? They will grow nearer home:

Grow nearer home – and out of the dream-house stumbling
One night into a strangling air and the flung
Rags of children and thunder of stone niagaras tumbling,
You'll know you slept too long.

c. 1938   C. DAY LEWIS

Different

Not to say what everyone else was saying
not to believe what everyone else believed
not to do what everybody did,
then to refute what everyone else was saying
then to disprove what everyone else believed
then to deprecate what everybody did,

was his way to come by understanding

how everyone else was saying the same as he was saying
believing what he believed
and did what doing

c. 1932   CLERE PARSONS

O for Doors to be Open

O for doors to be open and an invite with gilded edges
To dine with Lord Lobcock and Count Asthma on the plati-
    num benches,

With somersaults and fireworks, the roast and the smacking
  kisses –
        Cried the six cripples to the silent statue,
        The six beggared cripples.

And Garbo's and Cleopatra's wits to go astraying,
In a feather ocean with me to go fishing and playing,
Still jolly when the cock has burst himself with crowing –
        Cried the six cripples to the silent statue,
        The six beggared cripples.

And to stand on green turf among the craning yelling faces
Dependent on the chestnut, the sable, and Arabian horses,
And me with a magic crystal to foresee their places –
        Cried the six cripples to the silent statue,
        The six beggared cripples.

And this square to be a deck, and these pigeons sails to rig,
And to follow the delicious breeze like a tantony pig
To the shaded feverless islands where the melons are big –
        Cried the six cripples to the silent statue,
        The six beggared cripples.

And these shops to be turned to tulips in a garden bed,
And me with my crutch to thrash each merchant dead
As he pokes from a flower his bald and wicked head –
        Cried the six cripples to the silent statue,
        The six beggared cripples.

And a hole in the bottom of heaven, and Peter and Paul
And each smug surprised saint like parachutes to fall,
And every one-legged beggar to have no legs at all –
        Cried the six cripples to the silent statue,
        The six beggared cripples.

c. 1936   W. H. AUDEN

Bagpipe Music

It's no go the merry-go-round, it's no go the rickshaw,
All we want is a limousine and a ticket for the peepshow.
Their knickers are made of crêpe-de-chine, their shoes are
    made of python,
Their halls are lined with tiger rugs and their walls with
    heads of bison.

John MacDonald found a corpse, put it under the sofa,
Waited till it came to life and hit it with a poker,
Sold its eyes for souvenirs, sold its blood for whisky,
Kept its bones for dumb-bells to use when he was fifty.

It's no go the Yogi-Man, it's no go Blavatsky,
All we want is a bank balance and bit of a skirt in a taxi.

Annie MacDougall went to milk, caught her foot in the
    heather,
Woke to hear a dance record playing of Old Vienna.
It's no go your maidenheads, it's no go your culture,
All we want is a Dunlop tyre and the devil mend the
    puncture.

The Laird o'Phelps spent Hogmanay declaring he was sober,
Counted his feet to prove the fact and found he had one foot
    over.
Mrs Carmichael had her fifth, looked at the job with repul-
    sion,
Said to the midwife 'Take it away; I'm through with over-
    production'.

It's no go the gossip column, it's no go the Ceilidh,
All we want is a mother's help and a sugar-stick for the baby.

Willie Murray cut his thumb, couldn't count the damage,
Took the hide of an Ayrshire cow and used it for a bandage.
His brother caught three hundred cran when the seas were
   lavish,
Threw the bleeders back in the sea and went upon the parish.

It's no go the Herring Board, it's no go the Bible,
All we want is a packet of fags when our hands are idle.

It's no go the picture palace, it's no go the stadium,
It's no go the country cot with a pot of pink geraniums,
It's no go the Government grants, it's no go the elections,
Sit on your arse for fifty years and hang your hat on a pen-
   sion.

It's no go my honey love, it's no go my poppet;
Work your hands from day to day, the winds will blow the
   profit.
The glass is falling hour by hour, the glass will fall for ever,
But if you break the bloody glass you won't hold up the
   weather.

p. 1938   LOUIS MACNEICE

Missing Dates

Slowly the poison the whole blood stream fills.
It is not the effort nor the failure tires.
The waste remains, the waste remains and kills.

It is not your system or clear sight that mills
Down small to the consequence a life requires;
Slowly the poison the whole blood stream fills.

They bled an old dog dry yet the exchange rills
Of young dog blood gave but a month's desires;
The waste remains, the waste remains and kills.

It is the Chinese tombs and the slag hills
Usurp the soil, and not the soil retires.
Slowly the poison the whole blood stream fills.

Not to have fire is to be a skin that shrills.
The complete fire is death. From partial fires
The waste remains, the waste remains and kills.

It is the poems you have lost, the ills
From missing dates, at which the heart expires.
Slowly the poison the whole blood stream fills.
The waste remains, the waste remains and kills.

c. 1940   WILLIAM EMPSON

Slough

Come, friendly bombs, and fall on Slough
It isn't fit for humans now,
There isn't grass to graze a cow
      Swarm over, Death!

Come, bombs, and blow to smithereens
Those air-conditioned, bright canteens,
Tinned fruit, tinned meat, tinned milk, tinned beans
      Tinned minds, tinned breath.

Mess up the mess they call a town –
A house for ninety-seven down
And once a week a half a crown
      For twenty years,

And get that man with double chin
Who'll always cheat and always win,
Who washes his repulsive skin
      In women's tears.

And smash his desk of polished oak
And smash his hands so used to stroke
And stop his boring dirty joke
      And make him yell.

But spare the bald young clerks who add
The profits of the stinking cad;
It's not their fault that they are mad,
      They've tasted Hell.

It's not their fault they do not know
The birdsong from the radio,
It's not their fault they often go
      To Maidenhead.

And talk of sports and makes of cars
In various bogus Tudor bars
And daren't look up and see the stars
      But belch instead.

In labour-saving homes, with care
Their wives frizz out peroxide hair
And dry it in synthetic air
      And paint their nails.

Come, friendly bombs, and fall on Slough
To get it ready for the plough.
The cabbages are coming now:
      The earth exhales.

c. 1937   JOHN BETJEMAN

Beauty, Boloney

Cleopatra in her bath
had hair and soapsuds in her eyes;
I like Caligula's wrath
Cain's curses, Nero's ironies

Build me a temple of 90 pillars
a Sphinx, a Pyramid, with slaves;
the Parthenon's food for caterpillars
Britain's moneybags rule the waves

All the eagles and the trumpets
are daunted when Duke Ellington plays
beautiful strumpets beautiful crumpets
Eliot wronged the A.B.C.s

Paint me, Dali, if you will,
a landscape rich in bones and bread;
the Romance of Beecham's Pills
outlives Helen's maidenhead

True Beauty's in Nuffield and Ford
Mussolini, Chamberlain
they are the chosen of the Lord
let Laureates praise them, if they can

Let them scheme and gorge their fill
since beauty, said Renoir, must be fat:
we'll starve with Baudelaire in hell
Sade and Lautreamont share our fate

And we shall talk with Oscar Wilde
and all the Authors on the Index
while Rimbaud there shall, heartless child,
pull both of Edith Sitwell's legs

(yes, darling Jane shall be down there
as Matron of the Poet's Corner
but Pope and Dylan will take care
lest there be a plot to burn her)

But we are wandering from the subject
which was beauty : songs of larks
all winds, flowers and shrubs are suspect
we prefer the Brothers Marx

We prefer Modigliani
Klee and Braque and Picasso
to the Brutish Academy
(may Lewis deal its knock-out blow)

Lorca, Auden, Eluard
Cummings, MacNeice, Apollinaire
and Eliot are the giant hearts
slick, unvarnished, debonair

Meanwhile you can stuff the rest
in the British Museum
with fleas and laurels on their chest
polybourgeoism philodumb.

p. 1939   FRANCIS SCARFE

From *The New World This Hour Begets*

XI

If now the curtain dropped,
Would wonder, how we lacked,
Spite of all stage-effects,
Mere knowledge how to act.

Roads ribbing land and air
With maddening velocity
Have outrun mind's demesne,
Darkened a pointless sky.

Our guides withdrawn within
The soft elaborate rooms
Of memory, have there
Returned into time's womb.

Sterile of true creation
But subtle to destroy,
Their cautious drugs and thrills
Replace our active joy.

We shall not know again
That gorgeous flush of love,
Bringing the trophy home
Or dancing in the grove,

Until we dare unloose
The girdle of the heart,
Reveal how truly poor
We are, who seemed so smart.

Till our free spirit, waking
To its discovery, spans
This vacuum of purpose
And charges the itching hand.

It is time the late bud broke,
The leaves of love uncurled,
To submerge the whimpering self
Amid the living world,

To ride the storm, go on
And let the dead lament,
Expand the trade-routes, settle
New regions of content.

And love's first freedom find
In this its certain hour,
Bursting the dams, to loosen
The equal flood of power.

c. 1933   RANDALL SWINGLER

The Express

After the first powerful plain manifesto
The black statement of pistons, without more fuss
But gliding like a queen, she leaves the station.
Without bowing and with restrained unconcern
She passes the houses which humbly crowd outside,
The gasworks, and at last the heavy page
Of death, printed by gravestones in the cemetery.
Beyond the town there lies the open country
Where, gathering speed, she acquires mystery,
The luminous self-possession of ships on ocean.
It is now she begins to sing – at first quite low
Then loud, and at last with a jazzy madness –
The song of her whistle screaming at curves,
Of deafening tunnels, brakes, innumerable bolts.
And always light, aerial, underneath,
Retreats the elate metre of her wheels.
Steaming through metal landscape on her lines,
She plunges new eras of white happiness,
Where speed throws up strange shapes, broad curves
And parallels clean like the steel of guns.
At last, further than Edinburgh or Rome,
Beyond the crest of the world, she reaches night
Where only a low streamline brightness
Of phosphorus on the tossing hills is white.

Ah, like a comet through flame she moves entranced
Wrapt in her music no bird song, no, nor bough
Breaking with honey buds, shall ever equal.

p. 1932   STEPHEN SPENDER

Birmingham

Smoke from the train-gulf hid by hoardings blunders up-
ward, the brakes of cars
Pipe as the policeman pivoting round raises his flat hand,
bars
With his figure of monolith Pharaoh the queue of fidgety
machines
(Chromium dogs on the bonnet, faces behind the triplex
screens)
Behind him the streets run away between the proud glass of
shops
Cubical scent-bottles artificial legs arctic foxes and electric
mops
But beyond this centre the slumward vista thins like a dia-
gram:
There, unvisited, are Vulcan's forges who doesn't care a
tinker's damn.

Splayed outwards through the suburbs houses, houses for
rest
Seducingly rigged by the builder, half-timbered houses with
lips pressed
So tightly and eyes staring at the traffic through bleary haws
And only a six-inch grip of the racing earth in their con-
crete claws;
In these houses men as in a dream pursue the Platonic
Forms
With wireless and cairn terriers and gadgets approximating
to the fickle norms

And endeavour to find God and score one over the neigh-
   bour
By climbing tentatively upward on jerry-built beauty and
   sweated labour.

The lunch hour: the shops empty, shopgirls' faces relax
Diaphanous as green glass empty as old almanacs
As incoherent with ticketed gewgaws tiered behind their
   heads
As the Burne-Jones windows in St. Philip's broken by crawl-
   ing leads
Insipid colour, patches of emotion, Saturday thrills
'This theatre is sprayed with June' — the gutter take our
   old playbills,
Next week-end it is likely in the heart's funfair we shall pull
Strong enough on the handle to get back our money; or at
   any rate it is possible.

On shining lines the trams like vast sarcophagi move
Into the sky, plum after sunset, merging to duck's egg,
   barred with mauve
Zeppelin clouds, and pentecost-like the cars' headlights bud
Out from sideroads and the traffic signals, Crème-de-menthe
   or bull's blood,
Tell one to stop, the engine gently breathing, or to go on
To where like black pipes of organs in the frayed and fading
   zone
Of the West the factory chimneys on sullen sentry will all
   night wait
To call, in the harsh morning, sleep-stupid faces through the
   daily gate.

p. 1934   LOUIS MACNEICE

songs for swinging lovers

The Landscape near an Aerodrome

More beautiful and soft than any moth
With burring furred antennae feeling its huge path
Through dusk, the air-liner with shut-off engines
Glides over suburbs and the sleeves set trailing tall
To point the wind. Gently, broadly, she falls,
Scarcely disturbing charted currents of air.

Lulled by descent, the travellers across sea
And across feminine land indulging its easy limbs
In miles of softness, now let their eyes trained by watching
Penetrate through dusk the outskirts of this town
Here where industry shows a fraying edge.
Here they may see what is being done.

Beyond the winking masthead light
And the landing-ground, they observe the outposts
Of work: chimneys like lank black fingers
Or figures frightening and mad: and squat buildings
With their strange air behind trees, like women's faces
Shattered by grief. Here where few houses
Moan with faint light behind their blinds,
They remark the unhomely sense of complaint, like a dog
Shut out and shivering at the foreign moon.

In the last sweep of love, they pass over fields
Behind the aerodrome, where boys play all day
Hacking dead grass: whose cries, like wild birds
Settle upon the nearest roofs
But soon are hid under the loud city.

Then, as they land, they hear the tolling bell
Reaching across the landscape of hysteria,

To where larger than all the charcoaled batteries
And imaged towers against that dying sky,
Religion stands, the church blocking the sun.

c. 1933   STEPHEN SPENDER

At Richmond

At Richmond the river is running for the city:
Though the tall houses on the hill and hotels
In white paint hint of the cliffs and broader sea,
He cannot falter nor alter from his nature.
Lord, neither let falsity my days dissipate.
I have been weak and injudicious in many things,
Have made my tongue an irritant against my intention,
All quiet but a convalescence after sin,
And have frequently feared. Then forgive
Yet once, bless and beckon to the broken city.

w. 1939   ANNE RIDLER

Instructions

V

After the revolution, all that we have seen
Flitting as shadows on the flatness of the screen
Will stand out solid, will walk for all to touch
For doubters to thrust hands in and cry, yes, it is such.

The cells that have divided in our brains towards birth
The genetic characters of new heaven and new earth
These as warm bodies leaping out through the low door
Will laugh and shout and run, light now, lurking before.

The new world lying in ambush round the corner of time
Us waiting, eyes on the gauge, watching the mercury climb:
Till we hear on all lips a new song in the street all day,
Spreading from house to house without wires. This new
    song has come to stay.

We shall be differently aware, we shall see all things new
Not as a craze or a surprise, but hard, naked, true.
And trash heaped up, torn scraps, mud, all shall glow
    through and through
When the electric moment passes in, making them new.

Back of the streets and houses, back of all we had,
Back of our rooms, furniture, systems, words said,
The flow went on; we feel it now; the future was in our
    bones
And it springs out, bursts in drums, trumpets and saxo-
    phones.

It shines and we see it in the eyes and smiles of the stars,
It laughs in the newspapers and underground, plays in the
    headlights of cars,
In words it ripples and breaks in spray, and in rooms and in
    those we meet
Is lively, and in loving we find airways for feet.

p. 1933   CHARLES MADGE

Progression

See that Satan pollarding a tree,
That geometric man straightening a road:
Surely such passions are perverse and odd
That violate windows and set the north wind free.

No doubt tomorrow the world will be too straight,
Five hundred knots an hour will churn our dreams
Like surprised whales, when we lie a dead weight
In an ignorant sleep, and things will be what they seem.

Tomorrow we shall hear on the gramophone
The music of the Spheres, registered H.M.V.
By a divorced contralto: we shall perhaps
Meet Adam under glass in a museum
Fleshless and most unlovely, complete with pedigree.

Or else, tomorrow, workers kings and crooks
Will all have aeroplanes and be fast friends,
In a world no longer divided by dividends,
Where love will be almost as simple as it looks.

c. 1940   FRANCIS SCARFE

The Bells that Signed

The bells that signed a conqueror in
Or franked the lovers' bed, now mean
Nothing more heavenly than their
Own impulse and recoil of air.

But still at eve, when the wind swells
Out of the west, those rocking bells
Buoy up the sunken light, or mark
What rots unfathomed in the dark.

Broods the stone-lipped conqueror still
Abject upon his iron hill,
And lovers in the naked beds
Cry for more than maidenheads.

c. 1938   C. DAY LEWIS

Poems, XII

We made all possible preparations,
Drew up a list of firms,
Constantly revised our calculations
And allotted the farms,

Issued all the orders expedient
In this kind of case:
Most, as was expected, were obedient,
Though there were murmurs, of course;

Chiefly against our exercising
Our old right to abuse:
Even some sort of attempt at rising
But these were mere boys.

For never serious misgiving
Occurred to anyone,
Since there could be no question of living
If we did not win.

The generally accepted view teaches
That there was no excuse,
Though in the light of recent researches
Many would find the cause

In a not uncommon form of terror;
Others, still more astute,
Point to possibilities of error
At the very start.

As for ourselves there is left remaining
Our honour at least,
And a reasonable chance of retaining
Our faculties to the last.

c. 1930   W. H. AUDEN

Two Preludes

I

Died in action. This one killed at sea.
    A thousand dead in Ethiopa:
Recurring fractions of Thermopylae:
    The empire's grave, a new Matopa.

Caractacus had the people behind him,
    But the mob is no match for Rome.
Even Germanicus could not stem
    Onslaught on his home.

Caesar with a cocked hat and sword,
    Plumes for his generals and a microphone,
Can kill the silence with a hasty word.
    Young cadets will understand his tone.

2

Honour. And let us obey honour.
    Capital is at stake.
It is by popular clamour.
    The Punic war was not a fake.

The total of the man and state,
    Wived twice in a decade,
Decides transitory mandate
    And the right to raid.

Rumour. And rumours of war.
  Saved by a crucifix
From Caesar's sword, the Martyr
  Made no journey to the Styx.

p. 1937   H. B. MALLALIEU

Torch Song

The ring-fence aloofness
Of loved as loving richness,
Not designed for outside yes,
Admits no signal of distress;

Does not with the bankrupt know
How the shut mouth's steady no
Is the trap's refusal also,
Which growth will not overthrow.

The fence between here and here
Still separates mouth from ear
And good will cannot make clear
When hear is overhear.

From being too much said,
From being too much read,
The usual words are dead
And buried in the head.

While I try to draw the power
For an unconditional flower
From the synthetic our
Of a conversational hour

Always the dumb siege is stirred
By the mescal-eater's almost heard
Omnipotent transcendental word
To make why and because absurd

To build rhythms into one
To harness the latent sun
Plan out the work undone
Tell the blood how to run.

p. 1934   ROBERT HAMER

Sonnet

The brightness, the peculiar splendour
of sun on bark, the gleam of a single petal
varnished with light, or an old piece of tin
are always in the mind like points for lighting.

Burning like beacons bidding to the shore
are jointed things, or wood carefully sharpened,
moon in a pool, the dark source of a stream,
a dead mouse as though resting on moss.

Inalienable wealth the lightning eye
has given, and the conscious hand to keep,
to keep us moving, keep us guessing, safeguard
our slow steps in and out the ruined city
where already is ready to spring this heraldic lion,
the lynx-eyed evil of the dying order.

p. 1935   REX WARNER

Easter Monday

The corroded charred
Stems of iron town trees shoot pure jets
Of burning leaf. But the dust already
Quells their nervous flame: blowing from

The whitening spokes
Of wheels that flash away
And roar for Easter. The city is
A desert. Corinthian columns lie
Like chronicles of kings felled on their sides
And the acanthus leaf shoots other crowns
Of grass and moss. Sand and wires and glass
Glitter in empty, endless suns. . . . And
In the green meadows, girls in their first
Summer dresses, play. The hurdy-gurdy noise
Trumpets the valley, while egg-freckled arms
Weave their game, Children gather
Pap-swelling cowslips. Papers
Weightless as clouds, browse on the hills.
The bulls in tweeds
Hold in their golden spectacles
Twin crystal glasses, the velvet and far
Mountains. Look, holiday hands
From trams, 'buses, bicycles, and of tramps
Like one hand coarse with labour, grasp
The furred bloom of their peach.

p. 1935   STEPHEN SPENDER

New Year

Here at the centre of the turning year,
The turning Polar North,
The frozen streets and the black fiery joy
Of the Child launched again forth,
I ask that all the years and years
Of future disappointment, like a snow
Chide me at one fall now.

I leave him who burns endlessly
In the brandy pudding crowned with holly,
And I ask that Time should freeze my skin
And all my fellow travellers harden
Who are not flattered by this town
Nor up its twenty storeys whirled
To prostitutes without infection.

Cloak us in accidents and in the failure
Of the high altar and marital adventure;
In family disgrace, denunciation
Of bankers, a premier's assassination.
From the government windows
Let heads of headlines watch depart,
Strangely depart by staying, those
Who build a new world in their heart.

Where scythe shall curve but not upon our neck
And lovers proceed to their forgetting work
Answering the harvests of obliteration:
After the frozen years and streets
Our tempered Will shall plough across the nations.
This happy train that punishes no valley,
This hand that moves to make the silent lines,
Create their beauty without robbery.

p. 1934   STEPHEN SPENDER

II. THE LANDSCAPE WAS
THE OCCASION

Zennor

Seen from these cliffs the sea circles slowly.
  Ponderous and blue today, with waves furled,
  Slowly it crosses the curved world.
We wind in its waters with the tide,
  But the pendent ships afar
  Where the lightest blue and low clouds are
We lose as they hover and over the horizon slide.

When it was a dark blue heaven with foam like stars
  We saw it lean above us from the shore,
  And over the rocks the waves rear
Immense, and coming in with crests on fire;
  We could not understand,
  Finding the sea so high above the land,
What held its waters from flooding the world entire.

Today it lies in place, and the dun houses,
  The apple-green cloudy oats, the cows that seem
  Compact of the yellow crust of their cream,
Shrink on Amalveor's grey and tawny sides,
  Sucking the last shreds of sun.
  But all life here is carried on
Against the crash and cry of the moving tides.

w. 1939   ANNE RIDLER

The Secret Springs

Where are the secret springs, and where
The hidden source of sudden joy?
Whence is the laughter, like the torrent, falling? Whence
The tears, the rainbow-scattered sunlight, overhead?

Over the pinewood and the pasture and the pathway
Rises the rockface where the bootnails scratch
Smooth mossy walls, and the blind fingers reach
Damp ferns in crevices, and icy pools.

Water on brant and slape; the little streams
Rise in the gullies and the squelching moss:
Somewhere above the chockstone springs
Joy, and the sudden halt of tiny grief.

Summer will dry the rock-pool; winter bind
These, and the immortelles will bloom
In memory, and in memory only, these
Slow drops will fall.

Somewhere above the rockrose and the lichen,
Even in summer, or midwinter, moves
The powder-snow, the changing counterpart
Of changing, and unchanging, sea.

Somewhere above the step, the springs of action
Rise, and the snow falls, and the séracs; and the green
    glacier-ice
Moves down like history, or like the huge
Slow movement of a nation's mind.

Somewhere above the ice, unwitnessed storms
Break in the darkness on the summit ridge
And the white whirling avalanche
Blends with the storm, the night, the driven snow;

And sunlight, and the dark, and gravitation,
These are all: these are the hidden springs, simplicity,
And darkness is
The epitome of light, and darkness, and all lonely places.

c. 1936   MICHAEL ROBERTS

In September

Coming, in September, through the thin streets,
I thought back to another year I knew,
Autumn, lifting potatoes and stacking peats
On Mull, while the Atlantic's murky blue
Swung sluggishly in past Jura, and the hills
Were brown lions, crouched to meet the autumn gales.

In the hard rain and the rip of thunder,
I remembered the haze coming in from the sea
And the clatter of Gaelic voices by the breakwater
Or in the fields as the reapers took their tea;
I remembered the cast foal lying where it died,
Which we buried, one evening, above high-tide;

And the three rams that smashed the fank-gate,
Running loose for five days on the moor
Before we could catch them – far too late
To prevent an early lambing the next year.
But these seemed out of place beside the chip-shop
And the cockney voices grumbling in the pub.

In September, I saw the drab newsposters
Telling of wars, in Spain and in the East,
And wished I'd stayed on Mull, their gestures
Frightened me and made me feel the unwanted guest.
The burden on the house who having taken salt
Could never be ejected, however grave his fault.

In September, we lit the fire and talked together,
Discussing the trivialities of a spent day
And what we would eat. I forgot the weather

And the dull streets and the sun on Islay,
And all my fear. I lost my carefully-kept count
Of the ticks to death, and, in September, was content.

p. 1938   RUTHVEN TODD

Poem

Among these turf-stacks graze no iron horses
Such as stalk such as champ in towns and the soul of crowds,
Here is no mass-production of neat thoughts
No canvas shrouds for the mind nor any black hearses:
The peasant shambles on his boots like hooves
Without thinking at all or wanting to run in grooves.

But those who lack the peasant's conspirators,
The tawny mountain, the unregarded buttress,
Will feel the need of a fortress against ideas and against the
Shuddering insidious shock of the theory-vendors,
The little sardine men crammed in a monster toy
Who tilt their aggregate beast against our crumbling Troy.

For we are obsolete who like the lesser things
Who play in corners with looking-glass and beads;
It is better we should go quickly, go into Asia
Or any other tunnel where the world recedes,
Or turn blind wantons like the gulls who scream
And rip the edge off any ideal or dream.

p. 1933   LOUIS MACNEICE

Europe a Wood

The pattern is one of trees in precise formation,
Rubber or conifer, strictly utilitarian,
Uniform, without bud or blossom. Only the roots,
The trunk, the branches, some necessary leaves,
What is of use, and the power of propagation.

The motion is that of trees swaying in unison
To the prevailing wind. Bend or be broken.
Some fragmentary branches litter the ground,
Lopped from those trunks essayed a separate motion.
And upright trunks have crashed entire to earth.

The message is merely the speaking wind amplified:
That draught from a vacant space flutters the leaves
In the octave of assent, a murmured acceptance.
But of late, observers with sensitive ears report
Recalcitrant undertones, rustles of defiance.

p. 1938   GEOFFREY PARSONS

The Pylons

The secret of these hills was stone, and cottages
Of that stone made,
And crumbling roads
That turned on sudden hidden villages.

Now over these small hills they have built the concrete
That trails black wire:
Pylons, those pillars
Bare like nude, giant girls that have no secret.

The valley with its gilt and evening look
And the green chestnut
Of customary root,
Are mocked dry like the parched bed of a brook.

But far above and far as sight endures
Like whips of anger
With lightning's danger
There runs the quick perspective of the future.

This dwarfs our emerald country by its trek
So tall with prophecy:
Dreaming of cities
Where often clouds shall lean their swan-white neck.

c. 1933   STEPHEN SPENDER

From Feathers to Iron

14

Now the full-throated daffodils,
Our trumpeters in gold,
Call resurrection from the ground
And bid the year be bold.

Today the almond tree turns pink,
The first flush of the spring;
Winds loll and gossip through the town
Her secret whispering.

Now too the bird must try his voice
Upon the morning air;
Down drowsy avenues he cries
A novel great affair.

He tells of royalty to be;
How with her train of rose
Summer to coronation comes
Through waving wild hedgerows.

Today crowds quicken in a street
The fish leaps in the flood:
Look there, gasometer rises,
And here bough swells to bud.

For our love's luck, our stowaway,
Stretches in his cabin;
Our youngster joy barely conceived
Shows up beneath the skin.

Our joy was but a gusty thing
Without sinew or wit,
An infant flyaway; but now
We make a man of it.

c. 1931   C. DAY LEWIS

Sonnet

How sweet only to delight lambs and laugh by streams,
innocent in love wakening to the early thrush,
to be awed by mountains, and feel the stars friendly,
to be a farmer's boy, to be far from battle.

But me my blood binds to remember men
more than the birds, not to be delicate with squirrels,
or gloat among the poppies in a mass of corn,
or follow in a maze endless unwinding of water.

Nor will my mind permit me to linger in the love,
the mother kindness of country among ascending trees,
knowing that love must be liberated by bleeding,
fearing for my fellows, for the murder of man.

How should I live then but as a kind of fungus,
or else as one in strict training for desperate war?

c. 1937   REX WARNER

Place of Birth

From Winchester the road was dazed with heat
after the droughty downs the lanes were night
and drowned in leaves across their caky ruts:
down through the hedge's tunnel and the dust
lay my small village huddling in its trees.

Unmoved since twenty-two it's settled houses
however tiny to my later eyes
the fields the trees the bushes seemed the same
as when I left them in that dreaded April:
and though the men were dead or gone to Norwich
the women bedridden, the children married,
yet with the known road under my older feet
familiar cowsheds and remembered lanes
swooped back to me those misty years
when Hampshire was my home and London lovely.

The cottage squatted in its tangled garden
condemned for years to rot and sink;
the thatch was mossy and the well was rust
the hollow hogweed grew beside the barn
where the late sun was sitting through the cracks
and redhead docks stood in the living-room

against the curling paper on the wall
towards the ceiling's plaster and its stains:
I picked a plum from the forgotten tree
and wordless smells hung in the evening air
telling me I was eight, the school was finished,
through the long grass the twisty path, and home
was the small chimney down the valley's blue.

Here I was reared: these fields were mine for running
these beechy lanes my setting and my soil
a solemn boy with knees and canvas satchels . . .
the milkcan handle cold in Christmas snow
the plovers howling ghosts against the wind:
the larches in the copse were paintbox colours
and the red admirals hovered on the ivy:
the autumn brought its gleaning in the stubble
and apples drooping by the window pane.

This was my world, this unconsidered corner
and a long journey was a league away
through fields to Baybridge or to Fisher's Pond:
London was at the Pole, a kindly giant
with angel porters and tremendous trams:
and here I watched and walked, while vast unknown
history swept by, and blood in Ireland
war on the Soviets, Sacco in his gaol,
crisis, indemnities, putsches and revolts . . .
and I unseeing in my woods, happy in knowing
peace on the skyline and the future firm.

We weep for what is gone: my dying dog
is the pathetic puppy in the market cage;
never again that long oblivious calm
and yet our tears for loss, the dying years
the sun and colour of the spacious past:

and tonight's misty trees and mackerel sky
remembered in the draughty days to come
tearing at hearts shaken by midnight guns.

C. 1939   PETER HEWITT

Home Revisited

Now that I go there as a visitor,
To the end of the thin lane,
And pass the rockery with a stranger
Walk, I can recall his death again.

Birth and death identically change
While the house remains the same;
Grow from a boyhood's sword-sharp lunge
Of fear and love to an imagist's game.

Birth as the red-ribboning of a cot,
An unknown nurse in a rage;
As the seven swallows that sit
Dropping their pellets on the saxifrage

That wags its racket seed pods in the wind
Rotting brownly from the centre;
The doctor's shadow on the blind,
Spring summer autumn or winter.

Death as my walking past this empty shell:
The fixed memory of life
Ceasing like echoes in a well
Beyond the last ripple of short grief.

Death as a circle of nettles where the hut
Turned the patient to the wind.
That wind has taken seeds and set
Dock leaves' tusk roots into the heavy ground,

Or as the untidy nests the starlings build
To for ever leave and enter;
The doctor's shadow on the blind,
Spring summer autumn or winter.

p. 1939   BERNARD GUTTERIDGE

Allotments: April

Cobbled with rough stone which rings my tread
The path twists through the squared allotments.
Blinking to glimpse the lark in the warming sun,
In what sense am I joining in
Such a hallooing, rousing April day,
Now that the hedges are so gracious and
Stick out at me moist buds, small hands, their opening
  scrolls and fans?

Lost to some of us the festival joy
At the bursting of the tomb, the seasonal mystery,
God walking again who lay all winter
As if in those long barrows built in the fields
To keep the root-crops warm. On squires' lawns
The booted dancers twirl. But what I hear
Is spade slice in pebbled earth, swinging the nigger-coloured
  loam.

And the love-songs, the mediaeval grace,
The fluting lyrics, 'The only pretty ring-time',
These have stopped singing. For love detonates like sap
Up into the limbs of men and bears all the seasons
And the starving and the cutting and hunts terribly through
  lives
To find its peace. But April comes as
Beast-smell flung from the fields, the hammers, the loud-
  speaking weir.

The rough voices of boys playing by the hedge,
As manly as possible, their laughter, the big veins
Sprawled over the beet-leaf, light-red fires
Of flower pots heaped by the huts; they make a pause in
The wireless voice repeating pacts, persecutions,
And imprisonments and deaths and heaped violent deaths,
Impersonal now as figures in the city news.

Behind me, the town curves. Its parapeted edge,
With its burnt look, guards towards the river.
The worry about money, the eyeless work
Of those who do not believe, real poverty,
The sour doorways of the poor; April which
Delights the trees and fills the roads to the South,
Does not deny or conceal. Rather it adds

What more I am; excites the deep glands
And warms my animal bones as I go walking
Past the allotments and the singing water-meadows
Where hooves of cattle have plodded and cratered, and
Watch today go up like a single breath
Holding in its applause at masts of height
Two elms and their balanced attitude like dancers, their
   arms like dancers.

p. 1936   BERNARD SPENCER

Aisholt Revisited

These moors in August drank the burning sky,
And stretched out unslaked, scorched by gorse,
Though on either side ran the conduits of combe
With waving fronds and streams to the red loam
And appeasing pasture. I have known them too
When birds and water and the young green seemed

One element, the holly like tracks of a snail
Glittered in the soft new larch, and the combes were
  brindled
With primroses; or later in full May
Have looked at midday down into a mineral fire
Of blue and green in the woods, or at dusk descended
Where rhododendrons held the shrunk light like glass.
But ever Exmoor lay beautiful and hopelessly far
With unknown turrets and the named points.
I have visited these places at different times
With those I love most, and at each visit
Found a fissure from the past, that may not be
Taken up into the present, as it is in heaven,
And had, in the new pleasure, some sadness.
But I pray that the simplicity
And holiness of those days are not lost nor corrupted:
As we in these places still remember Wordsworth,
At Alfoxton consider how he could run that huge house,
See where he walked with Coleridge, and the places are
  holy.
That was unaltered, though he grew old and stiff,
Though Coleridge was impossible in a house,
And Dorothy's brain grew soft by the fire.
The landscape was the occasion and the vessel.
So let our times by the living streams,
In the secret cottage, or in the curled combes,
Be taken up into Godhead, and be for ever.

w. 1939   ANNE RIDLER

III. TO WALK WITH OTHERS

I Think Continually

I think continually of those who were truly great.
Who, from the womb, remembered the soul's history
Through corridors of light where the hours are suns
Endless and singing. Whose lovely ambition
Was that their lips, still touched with fire,
Should tell of the Spirit clothed from head to foot in song.
And who hoarded from the Spring branches
The desires falling across their bodies like blossoms.

What is precious, is never to forget
The essential delight of the blood drawn from ageless springs
Breaking through rocks in worlds before our earth.
Never to deny its pleasure in the morning simple light
Nor its grave evening demand for love.
Never to allow gradually the traffic to smother
With noise and fog the flowering of the Spirit.

Near the snow, near the sun, in the highest fields
See how these names are fêted by the waving grass
And by the streamers of white cloud
And whispers of wind in the listening sky.
The names of those who in their lives fought for life,
Who wore at their hearts the fire's centre.
Born of the sun they travelled a short while toward the sun
And left the vivid air signed with their honour.

c. 1933   STEPHEN SPENDER

Lament for a Cricket Eleven

Beyond the edge of the sepia
Rises the weak photographer
With the moist moustaches and the made-up tie.
He looked with his mechanical eye,
And the upshot was that they had to die.

Portrait of the Eleven nineteen-o-five
To show when these missing persons were last alive.
Two sit in Threadneedle Street like gnomes.
One is a careless schoolmaster
Busy with carved desks, honour and lines.
He is eaten by a wicked cancer.
They have detectives to watch their homes.

From the camera hood he looks at the faces
Like the spectral pose of the praying mantis.
Watch for the dicky-bird. But, oh my dear,
That bird will not migrate this year.
Oh for a parasol, oh for a fan
To hide my weak chin from the little man.

One climbs mountains in a storm of fear,
Begs to be unroped and left alone.
One went mad by a tape-machine.
One laughed for a fortnight and went to sea.
Like a sun one follows the jeunesse dorée.

With his hand on the bulb he looks at them.
The smiles on their faces are upside down.
'I'll turn my head and spoil the plate.'
'Thank you, gentlemen.' Too late, too late.

One greyhead was beaten in a prison riot.
He needs injections to keep him quiet.
Another was a handsome clergyman,
But mortification has long set in.
One keeps six dogs in an unlit cellar.
The last is a randy bachelor.

The photographer in the norfolk jacket
Sits upstairs in his darkroom attic.
His hand is expert at scissors and pin.
The shadows lengthen, the days draw in
And the mice come out round the iron stove.
'What I am doing, I am doing for love.
When shall I burn this negative
And hang the receiver up on grief?'

p. 1938   KENNETH ALLOTT

A Carol

Oh hush thee, my baby,
Thy cradle's in pawn:
No blankets to cover thee
Cold and forlorn.
The stars in the bright sky
Look down and are dumb
At the heir of the ages
Asleep in a slum.

The hooters are blowing,
No heed let him take;
When baby is hungry
'Tis best not to wake.

E   113

Thy mother is crying,
Thy dad's on the dole:
Two shillings a week is
The price of a soul.

c. 1935

C. DAY LEWIS

Carol

There was a Boy bedded in bracken
Like to a sleeping snake all curled he lay
On his thin navel turned this spinning sphere
Each feeble finger fetched seven suns away
He was not dropped in good-for-lambing weather
He took no suck when shook buds sing together
But he is come in cold-as-workhouse weather
Poor as a Salford child.

p. 1936

JOHN SHORT

The Child

How can I teach, how can I save,
This child whose features are my own,
Whose feet run down the ways where I have walked?

How can I name that vision past the corner,
How warn the seed that grows to constant anger,
How can I draw the map that tells no lies?

His world is a small world of hours and minutes,
Hedgerows shut in the horizons of his thought,
His loves are uncritical and deep,
His anger innocent and sudden like a minnow.

His eyes, acute and quick, are unprotected,
Unsandalled still, his feet run down the lane,
Down to that lingering horror in the brambles,
The limp crashed airman, in the splintered goggles.

c. 1939   MICHAEL ROBERTS

The Token

More beautiful than any gift you gave
You were, a child so beautiful as to seem
To promise ruin what no child can have
Or woman give. And so a Roman gem
I choose to be your token: here a laurel
Springs to its young height, hangs a broken limb.
And here a group of women wanly quarrel
At a sale of Cupids. A hawk looks at them.

c. 1938   F. T. PRINCE

Death of King George V

'New King arrives in his capital by air . . .'
Daily Newspaper

Spirits of well-shot woodcock, partridge, snipe
    Flutter and bear him up the Norfolk sky:
In that red house in a red mahogany book-case
    The stamp collection waits with mounts long dry.

The big blue eyes are shut which saw wrong clothing
    And favourite fields and coverts from a horse;
Old men in country houses hear clocks ticking
    Over thick carpets with a deadened force;

115

Old men who never cheated, never doubted,
  Communicated monthly, sit and stare
At the new suburb stretched beyond the run-way
  Where a young man lands hatless from the air.

c. 1937   JOHN BETJEMAN

Resort

Ageless men, behind terraces,
Glance over geraniums,
Calling for Vichy water
In the long afternoons.

Girls, as tender as cats for milk,
Are framed in doorways
Decorating their small tight cheeks
In clots and dabs.

Men and girls are coupled
By painted fingernails
By car cushions
By the new tune called 'Love'.

w. 1934   JOHN PUDNEY

Reginal Order

Slow swell of walk insists
'I'm woman'; suggests
Hot spheres of flesh.

Uvula'd talk lifts lip
From new-licked smile.
Lids close to a slit.

Creates thick lust
This radioactive she,
Bids man be brisk.

p. 1933   GEOFFREY GRIGSON

To an Old Lady

Ripeness is all; her in her cooling planet
Revere; do not presume to think her wasted.
Project her no projectile, plan nor man it;
Gods cool in turn, by the sun long outlasted.

Our earth alone given no name of god
Gives, too, no hold for such a leap to aid her;
Landing, you break some palace and seem odd;
Bees sting their need, the keeper's queen invader.

No, to your telescope; spy out the land;
Watch while her ritual is still to see,
Still stand her temples emptying in the sand
Whose waves o'erthrew their crumbled tracery;

Still stand uncalled-on her soul's appanage;
Much social detail whose successor fades,
Wit used to run a house and to play Bridge,
And tragic fervour, to dismiss her maids.

Years her precession do not throw from gear.
She reads a compass certain of her pole;
Confident, finds no confines on her sphere,
Whose failing crops are in her sole control.

Stars how much further from me fill my night,
Strange that she too should be inaccessible,
Who shares my sun. He curtains her from sight,
And but in darkness is she visible.

c. 1935   WILLIAM EMPSON

On a Portrait of a Deaf Man

The kind old face, the egg-shaped head
    The tie, discreetly loud,
The loosely fitting shooting clothes,
    A closely fitting shroud.

He liked Old City dining-rooms,
    Potatoes in their skin,
But now his mouth is wide to let
    The London clay come in.

He took me on long silent walks
    In country lanes when young,
He knew the name of ev'ry bird
    But not the song it sung.

And when he could not hear me speak
    He smiled and looked so wise
That now I do not like to think
    Of maggots in his eyes.

He liked the rain-washed Cornish air
    And smell of ploughed-up soil,
He liked a landscape big and bare
    And painted it in oil.

But least of all he liked that place
    Which hangs on Highgate Hill
Of soaked Carrara-covered earth
    For Londoners to fill.

He would have liked to say good-bye,
    Shake hands with many friends,
In Highgate now his finger-bones
    Stick through his finger-ends.

You, God, who treat him thus and thus,
  Say 'Save his soul and pray.'
You ask me to believe You and
  I only see decay.

c. 1940   JOHN BETJEMAN

Epitaph for a Riveter

There need be no haste, slowly bear
Him along by the tenements;
He will never give heed to the Metro
Crisply accelerating below the fence.

Womb's entourage gave him small respite
From the forensic bark of punctual steel:
Expend no curses on the pathogen
That stars him in his last newsreel.

p. 1933   RONALD BOTTRALL

The Collier

When I was born on Amman hill
A dark bird crossed the sun.
Sharp on the floor the shadow fell;
I was the youngest son.

And when I went to the County School
I worked in a shaft of light.
In the wood of the desk I cut my name:
Dai for Dynamite.

The tall black hills my brothers stood;
Their lessons all were done.
From the door of the school when I ran out
They frowned to watch me run.

The slow grey bells they rung a chime
Surly with grief or age.
Clever or clumsy, lad or lout,
All would look for a wage.

I learnt the valley flowers' names
And the rough bark knew my knees.
I brought home trout from the river
And spotted eggs from the trees.

A coloured coat I was given to wear
Where the lights of the rough land shone.
Still jealous of my favour
The tall black hills looked on.

They dipped my coat in the blood of a kid
And they cast me down a pit,
And although I crossed with strangers
There was no way up from it.

Soon as I went from the County School
I worked in a shaft. Said Jim,
'You will get your chain of gold, my lad,
But not for a likely time.'

And one said, 'Jack was not raised up
When the wind blew out the light
Though he interpreted their dreams
And guessed their fears by night.'

And Tom, he shivered his leper's lamp
For the stain that round him grew;
And I heard mouths pray in the after-damp
When the picks would not break through.

They changed words there in darkness
And still through my head they run,
And white on my limbs is the linen sheet
And gold on my neck the sun.

w. 1937–8   VERNON WATKINS

Death in Leamington

She died in the upstairs bedroom
  By the light of the ev'ning star
That shone through the plate-glass window
  From over Leamington Spa.

Beside her the lonely crochet
  Lay patiently and unstirred,
But the fingers that would have work'd it
  Were dead as the spoken word.

And Nurse came in with the tea-things
  Breast high 'mid the stands and chairs –
But Nurse was alone with her own little soul,
  And the things were alone with theirs.

She bolted the big round window,
  She let the blinds unroll,
She set a match to the mantle,
  She covered the fire with coal.

And 'Tea!' she said in a tiny voice
  'Wake up! It's nearly *five*.'
Oh! Chintzy, chintzy cheeriness,
  Half dead and half alive!

Do you know that the stucco is peeling?
  Do you know that the heart will stop?
From those yellow Italianate arches
  Do you hear the plaster drop?

Nurse looked at the silent bedstead,
　　At the grey, decaying face,
As the calm of a Leamington ev'ning
　　Drifted into the place.

She moved the table of bottles
　　Away from the bed to the wall;
And tiptoeing gently over the stairs
　　Turned down the gas in the hall.

c. 1932　　　　　　　　　　　　　　　JOHN BETJEMAN

In Memory of Ann Jones

After the funeral, mule praises, brays,
Windshake of sailshaped ears, muffle-toed tap
Tap happily of one peg in the thick
Grave's foot, blinds down the lids, the teeth in black,
The spittled eyes, the salt ponds in the sleeves,
Morning smack of the spade that wakes up sleep,
Shakes a desolate boy who slits his throat
In the dark of the coffin and sheds dry leaves,
That breaks one bone to light with a judgment clout,
After the feast of tear-stuffed time and thistles
In a room with a stuffed fox and a stale fern,
I stand, for this memorial's sake, alone
In the snivelling hours with dead, humped Ann
Whose hooded, fountain heart once fell in puddles
Round the parched worlds of Wales and drowned each sun
(Though this for her is a monstrous image blindly
Magnified out of praise; her death was a still drop;
She would not have me sinking in the holy
Flood of her heart's fame; she would lie dumb and deep
And need no druid of her broken body).
But I, Ann's bard on a raised hearth, call all

The seas to service that her wood-tongued virtue
Babble like a bell-buoy over the hymning heads,
Bow down the walls of the ferned and foxy woods
That her love sing and swing through a brown chapel,
Bless her bent spirit with four, crossing birds.
Her flesh was meek as milk, but this skyward statue
With the wild breast and blessed and giant skull
Is carved from her in a room with a wet window
In a fiercely mourning house in a crooked year.
I know her scrubbed and sour humble hands
Lie with religion in their cramp, her threadbare
Whisper in a damp word, her wits drilled hollow,
Her fist of a face died clenched on a round pain;
And sculptured Ann is seventy years of stone.
These cloud-sopped, marble hands, this monumental
Argument of the hewn voice, gesture and psalm
Storm me forever over her grave until
The stuffed lung of the fox twitch and cry Love
And the strutting fern lay seeds on the black sill.

c. 1939   DYLAN THOMAS

Part of Plenty

When she carries food to the table and stoops down
– Doing this out of love – and lays soup with its good
Tickling smell, or fry winking from the fire
And I look up, perhaps from a book I am reading
Or other work: there is an importance of beauty
Which can't be accounted for by there and then,
And attacks me, but not separately from the welcome
Of the food, or the grace of her arms.

When she puts a sheaf of tulips in a jug
And pours in water and presses to one side
The upright stems and leaves that you hear creak,

Or loosens them, or holds them up to show me,
So that I see the tangle of their necks and cups
With the curls of her hair, and the body they are held
Against, and the stalk of the small waist rising
And flowering in the shape of breasts;

Whether in the bringing of the flowers or the food
She offers plenty, and is part of plenty,
And whether I see her stooping, or leaning with the flowers,
What she does is ages old, and she is not simply,
No, but lovely in that way.

p. 1937   BERNARD SPENCER

The British Museum Reading Room

Under the hive-like dome the stooping haunted readers
Go up and down the alleys, tap the cells of knowledge –
    Honey and wax, the accumulation of years . . .
Some on commission, some for the love of learning,
Some because they have nothing better to do
Or because they hope these walls of books will deaden
    The drumming of the demon in their ears.

Cranks, hacks, poverty-stricken scholars,
In pince-nez, period hats or romantic beards
    And cherishing their hobby or their doom,
Some are too much alive and some are asleep
Hanging like bats in a world of inverted values,
Folded up in themselves in a world which is safe and silent:
    This is the British Museum Reading Room.

Out on the steps in the sun the pigeons are courting,
Puffing their ruffs and sweeping their tails or taking
    A sun-bath at their ease

And under the totem poles – the ancient terror –
Between the enormous fluted Ionic columns
There seeps from heavily jowled or hawk-like foreign faces
  The guttural sorrow of the refugees.

July, 1939   LOUIS MACNEICE

And Forgetful of Europe
(Mlina 1935 to 1937)

Think now about all the things which made up
That place: you noticed first
Under the plane tree, where the red
And white canoes were, the green peppers
And the black figs on the stall: the countess then
(slightly red when we came close
Between the brown of her body
And her white bathing dress),
Her blonde hair pulled off her smart
Old face, her crimson nails, and not
A quiver in the guarded bust, as she rose
With Bull-dog Drummond from her wicker
Chair: then from the Countess
To the chapel, under the pink and the white
Oleanders, up the path between the white walls
And the soft agrimony: the orchard with
Scarlet pomegranate flowers, the very deep
Stream full of light in its curved
Silk-stocking-coloured limestone bed.
A sulphur wagtail balanced, where it moved
Under the mill-house.
                   And then came
The first fall, where the water bellied out
Over a limestone hood (remember, my darling,

The cave behind the hood, and the way
The limestone coated the roots of the trees there):
And the second fall seen for a dinar,
So high the water just poured from
The intensest heaven, through the figs on the lime-
Stone precipice.

              I think there were doves
Sounding among the figs. Certainly
There were swallows all around, more
Wagtails, and two black and white
Dippers there.

              And when we came down
Again through the leaves it was obvious
That the chapel tower was new, that
The stones were machine-cut and too regular;
But then the sun was going down
Behind Cavtat: the sea turned a quieter blue
Crossed with catches of yellow, and
The pink and white of those two vast
Oleanders caught just the slight china-
Tea colour of the sun.

How we were hungry then: how we felt
We enjoyed the fish, the olives, and the chocolate
Cake, under the miniature emerald grapes!
How vigorously we talked of nothing with
The countess and old white and pink and
Wicked Strozzi! How we enjoyed our bridge with
    them,
The scarlet nails drumming *Tisch, Tisch,*
When the lead was wrong! And after
Our two rubbers at ten dinars
A hundred, you and I fifty dinars and
Five hundred to the bad, how we marked
The lights of the fish-spearers and wished

There was a moon over the cypresses,
And forgetful of Europe, walked to bed
In the warm wind from the mountain.

p. 1938   GEOFFREY GRIGSON

Public-House Confidence

Well, since you're from the other side of town,
I'll tell you how I hold a soft job down,
In the designing-rooms and laboratory
I'm dressed in overalls, and so pretend
To be on business from the factory.
The workmen think I'm from the other end.
The in-betweens and smart commission-men
Believe I must have some pull with the boss.
So, playing off the spanner against the pen
I never let the rumour get across
Of how I am no use at all to either
And draw the pay of both for doing neither.

p. 1933   NORMAN CAMERON

In Westminster Abbey

Let me take this other glove off
    As the *vox humana* swells,
And the beauteous fields of Eden
    Bask beneath the Abbey bells.
Here, where England's statesmen lie,
Listen to a lady's cry.

Gracious Lord, oh bomb the Germans.
    Spare their women for Thy Sake,
And if that is not too easy
    We will pardon Thy Mistake.
But, gracious Lord, whate'er shall be,
Don't let anyone bomb me.

Keep our Empire undismembered
    Guide our Forces by Thy Hand,
Gallant blacks from far Jamaica,
    Honduras and Togoland;
Protect them Lord in all their fights,
And, even more, protect the whites.

Think of what our Nation stands for,
    Books from Boots and country lanes,
Free speech, free passes, class distinction,
    Democracy and proper drains.
Lord, put beneath Thy special care
One-eighty-nine Cadogan Square.

Although dear Lord I am a sinner,
    I have done no major crime;
Now I'll come to Evening Service
    Whensoever I have the time.
So, Lord, reserve for me a crown.
And do not let my shares go down.

I will labour for Thy Kingdom,
    Help our lads to win the war,
Send white feathers to the cowards
    Join the Women's Army Corps,
Then wash the Steps around Thy Throne
In the Eternal Safety Zone.

Now I feel a little better,
  What a treat to hear Thy word,
Where the bones of leading statesmen,
  Have so often been interr'd.
And now, dear Lord, I cannot wait
Because I have a luncheon date.

c. 1940   JOHN BETJEMAN

Sea Dirge

I was not particularly anxious for marine adventure,
the shore had cast me off. One night
moonless, a Hesperus affair, the deluge rose,
licked me, and sucked me down. The maw
of salt and sand decided on my fate.
I lie below these waves. The consulate
of death is certain, and I make no protest;
save that the ribs of galleons are not found,
but skulls and common fish and no romance.

c. 1938   EDGAR FOXALL

IV. AND I REMEMBER SPAIN

Spain

Yesterday all the past. The language of size
Spreading to China along the trade-routes; the diffusion
      Of the counting-frame and the cromlech;
Yesterday the shadow-reckoning in the sunny climates.

Yesterday the assessment of insurance by cards,
The divination of water; yesterday the invention
      Of cartwheels and clocks, the taming of
Horses. Yesterday the bustling world of the navigators.

Yesterday the abolition of fairies and giants,
The fortress like a motionless eagle eyeing the valley,
      The chapel built in the forest;
Yesterday the carving of angels and alarming gargoyles.

The trial of heretics among the columns of stone;
Yesterday the theological feuds in the taverns
      And the miraculous cure at the fountain;
Yesterday the Sabbath of witches; but to-day the struggle.

Yesterday the installation of dynamos and turbines,
The construction of railways in the colonial desert;
      Yesterday the classic lecture
On the origin of Mankind. But to-day the struggle.

Yesterday the belief in the absolute value of Greece,
The fall of the curtain upon the death of a hero;
      Yesterday the prayer to the sunset
And the adoration of madmen. But to-day the struggle.

As the poet whispers, startled among the pines,
Or where the loose waterfall sings compact, or upright
      On the crag by the leaning tower:
'O my vision. O send me the luck of the sailor.'

And the investigator peers through his instruments
At the inhuman provinces, the virile bacillus
      Or enormous Jupiter finished:
'But the lives of my friends. I inquire. I inquire.'

And the poor in their fireless lodgings, dropping the sheets
Of the evening paper: 'Our day is our loss, O show us
      History the operator, the
Organizer, Time the refreshing river.'

And the nations combine each cry, invoking the life
That shapes the individual belly and orders
      The private nocturnal terror:
'Did you not found the city state of the sponge,

'Raise the vast military empires of the shark
And the tiger, establish the robin's plucky canton?
      Intervene. O descend as a dove or
A furious papa or a mild engineer, but descend.'

And the life, if it answers at all, replies from the heart
And the eyes and the lungs, from the shops and squares of
  the city:
      'O no, I am not the mover;
Not to-day; not to you. To you, I'm the

'Yes-man, the bar-companion, the easily-duped;
I am whatever you do. I am your vow to be
      Good, your humorous story.
I am your business voice. I am your marriage.

'What's your proposal? To build the just city? I will.
I agree. Or is it the suicide pact, the romantic
     Death? Very well, I accept, for
I am your choice, your decision. Yes, I am Spain.'

Many have heard it on remote peninsulas,
On sleepy plains, in the aberrant fisherman's islands
     Or the corrupt heart of the city,
Have heard and migrated like gulls or the seeds of a flower.

They clung like birds to the long expresses that lurch
Through the unjust lands, through the night, through the
   alpine tunnel;
     They floated over the oceans;
They walked the passes. All presented their lives.

On that arid square, that fragment nipped off from hot
Africa, soldered so crudely to inventive Europe;
     On that tableland scored by rivers,
Our thoughts have bodies; the menacing shapes of our
   fever

Are precise and alive. For the fears which made us respond
To the medicine ad, and the brochure of winter cruises
     Have become invading battalions;
And our faces, the institute-face, the chain-store, the ruin

Are projecting their greed as the firing squad and the bomb.
Madrid is the heart. Our moments of tenderness blossom
     As the ambulance and the sandbag;
Our hours of friendship into a people's army.

To-morrow, perhaps the future. The research on fatigue
And the movement of packers; the gradual exploring of all
   the
     Octaves of radiation;
To-morrow the enlarging of consciousness by diet and
   breathing.

To-morrow the rediscovery of romantic love,
The photographing of ravens; all the fun under
        Liberty's masterful shadow;
To-morrow the hour of the pageant-master and the musician,

The beautiful roar of the chorus under the dome;
To-morrow the exchanging of tips on the breeding of terriers,
        The eager election of chairmen
By the sudden forest of hands. But to-day the struggle.

To-morrow for the young poets exploding like bombs,
The walks by the lake, the weeks of perfect communion;
        To-morrow the bicycle races
Through the suburbs on summer evenings. But to-day the
    struggle.

To-day the deliberate increase in the chances of death,
The conscious acceptance of guilt in the necessary murder;
        To-day the expending of powers
On the flat ephemeral pamphlet and the boring meeting.

To-day the makeshift consolations: the shared cigarette,
The cards in the candlelit barn, and the scraping concert,
        The masculine jokes; to-day the
Fumbled and unsatisfactory embrace before hurting.

The stars are dead. The animals will not look.
We are left alone with our day, and the time is short, and
        History to the defeated
May say alas but cannot help or pardon.

c. 1937   W. H. AUDEN

Full Moon at Tierz: Before the
Storming of Huesca

1

The past, a glacier, gripped the mountain wall,
And time was inches, dark was all.
But here it scales the end of the range,
The dialectic's point of change,
Crashes in light and minutes to its fall.

Time present is a cataract whose force
Breaks down the banks even at its source
And history forming in our hand's
Not plasticine but roaring sands,
Yet we must swing it to its final course.

The intersecting lines that cross both ways,
Time future, has no image in space,
Crooked as the road that we must tread,
Straight as our bullets fly ahead.
We are the future. The last fight let us face.

2

Where, in the fields by Huesca, the full moon
Throws shadows clear as daylight's, soon
The innocence of this quiet plain
Will fade in sweat and blood, in pain,
As our decisive hold is lost or won.

All round the barren hills of Aragon
Announce our testing has begun.
Here what the Seventh Congress said,
If true, if false, is live or dead,
Speaks in the Oviedo mauser's tone.

Three years ago Dimitrov fought alone
And we stood taller when he won.
But now the Leipzig dragon's teeth
Sprout strong and handsome against death
And here an army fights where there was one.

We studied well how to begin this fight,
Our Maurice Thorez held the light.
But now by Monte Aragon
We plunge into the dark alone,
Earth's newest planet wheeling through the night.

*To boldly go where no Man
has gone before.*

3

Though Communism was my waking time,
Always before the lights of home
Shone clear and steady and full in view —
Here, if you fall, there's help for you —
Now, with my Party, I stand quite alone.

Then let my private battle with my nerves,
The fear of pain whose pain survives,
The love that tears me by the roots,
The loneliness that claws my guts,
Fuse in the welded front our fight preserves.

O be invincible as the strong sun,
Hard as the metal of my gun,
O let the mounting tempo of the train
Sweep where my footsteps slipped in vain,
October in the rhythm of its run.

4

Now the same night falls over Germany
And the impartial beauty of the stars
Lights from the unfeeling sky

Oranienburg and freedom's crooked scars.
We can do nothing to ease that pain
But prove the agony was not in vain.

England is silent under the same moon,
From the Clydeside to the gutted pits of Wales.
The innocent mask conceals that soon
Here, too, our freedom's swaying in the scales.
O understand before too late
Freedom was never held without a fight.

Freedom is an easily spoken word
But facts are stubborn things. Here, too, in Spain
Our fight's not won till the workers of all the world
Stand by our guard on Huesca's plain
Swear that our dead fought not in vain,
Raise the red flag triumphantly
For Communism and for liberty.

w. 1936   JOHN CORNFORD

The Times

Time wasted and time spent
Daytime with used up wit
Time to stand, time to sit
Or wait and see if it
Happens, happy event.

For war is eating now

Waking, shaking of death
Leaving the white sheets
And dull head who repeats
The dream of his defeats
And drawing colder breath

For war is eating now.

Growing older, going
Where the water runs
Black as death, and guns
Explode the sinking suns
Blowing like hell, snowing

For war is eating now. Digger Murdo

p. 1933   CHARLES MADGE

Prize for Good Conduct

Will you take a seat?
                    The War will soon be over.
The state requires
                    my wedding ring and my apostle spoons
                    my sons.

There will be a special service in the cathedral
after which the clergy will be disbanded
and the fane profaned and put to immediate service
to manufacture wooden legs for heroes
with a profitable side-line in glass-eyes
and employment found for over two hundred widows.

The feverish wounded in the base hospital
the nurse's coif becomes a phallic symbol
he hears the red cool drop and the cistern filling;
and the stripped dead buried in ungainly postures
their lucky charms sent back with kindly letters;
the invalids sent home with eyesight failing
to sit on a waiting list for operations
and never to be put off iron rations;

and the nervous shipwrecked bodies in lovely grounds
set aside by old ladies with unearned incomes,
crucified nerves which come to life obliquely:
the cows are licking the shadow from the field
the wasps buzz angrily in the stoppered bottle
the devil comes daintily over the stepping stones
they sit in the sunshine, crying no rest for the wicked.

p. 1936   KENNETH ALLOTT

A Thousand Killed

I read of a thousand killed.
And am glad because the scrounging imperial paw
Was there so bitten:
As a man at elections is thrilled
When the results pour in, and the North goes with him
And the West breaks in the thaw.

(That fighting was a long way off.)

Forgetting therefore an election
Being fought with votes and lies and catch-cries
And orator's frowns and flowers and posters' noise,
Is paid for with cheques and toys:
Wars the most glorious
Victory-winged and steeple-uproarious
. . . With the lives, burned-off,
Of young men and boys.

p. 1936   BERNARD SPENCER

Poem

He awoke from dreams of the fortunate isles,
waters heavy with unaccustomed fish,
olive and cyprus down the exciting bank
and phallic sneers in harbour lights;
it was day already, the morning roll
fresh on the plate, the paper folded.

Where are those isles? Oh, the war in Spain,
and torrents waiting to fall from the sky;
the pressed trousers and the perfect part
in the thin hair of the a.m. nuisance.
All the blonde typists with hot legs
and minds like turkeys, birds with mean eyes.

Lower the sky to spire, the church to rot,
let the bell ring the fat to warm bath,
draped bone and muscular impotence reborn
in the Monday world without end. O white
gangrene of certainty like the dead park,
all the embittered foliage of peace.

c. 1938   EDGAR FOXALL

The Non-Interveners

In England the handsome Minister with the second
and a half chin and his heart-shaped mind
hanging on his thin watch-chain, the Minister
with gout who shaves low on his holly-stem neck.

In Spain still the brown and gilt and the twisted
pillar, still the olives, and in the mountains
the chocolate trunks of cork trees bare from

the knee, the little smoke from the sides
of the charcoal-burner's grey tump, the ebony sea-
hedgehogs in the clear water, the cuttle speared
at night; and also the black slime under
the bullet-pocked wall, also the arterial blood
squirting into the curious future, also
the greasy cloud streaked with red in yellow: and,

In England, the ominous grey paper, with its
indifferent headline, its news from our own
correspondent away from the fighting;
and in England the crack-willows, their
wet leaves reversed by the wind; and
the swallows sitting different ways like
notes of music between the black poles on
the five telephone wires.

w. 1937   GEOFFREY GRIGSON

A Cold Night

Thick wool is muslin to-night, and the wire
Wind scorches stone-cold colder. Boys
Tremble at counters of shops. The world
Gets lopped at the radius of my fire.

Only for a moment I think of those
Whom the weather leans on under the sky;
Newsmen with placards by the river's skirt,
Stamping, or with their crouching pose,

The whores; the soldiery who lie
Round wounded Madrid; those of less hurt
Who cross that bridge I crossed today
Where the waves snap white as broken plates

And the criss-cross girders hammer a grill
Through which, instead of flames, wind hates.

I turn back to my fire. Which I must.
I am not God or a crazed woman.
And one needs time too to sit in peace
Opposite one's girl, with food, fire, light,

And do the work one's own blood heats,
Or talk, and forget about the winter,
– This season, this century – and not be always
Opening one's doors on the pitiful streets

Of Europe, not always think of winter, winter, like a
    hammering rhyme
For then everything is drowned by the rising wind,
    everything is done against Time.

p. 1937   BERNARD SPENCER

Two Armies

Deep in the winter plain, two armies
Dig their machinery, to destroy each other.
Men freeze and hunger. No one is given leave
On either side, except the dead, and wounded.
These have their leave; while new battalions wait
On time at last to bring them violent peace.

All have become so nervous and so cold
That each man hates the cause and distant words
Which brought him here, more terribly than bullets.
Once a boy hummed a popular marching song,

STEPHEN SPENDER

Once a novice hand flapped the salute;
The voice was choked, the lifted hand fell,
Shot through the wrist by those of his own side.

From their numb harvest all would flee, except
For discipline drilled once in an iron school
Which holds them at the point of a revolver.
Yet when they sleep, the images of home
Ride wishing horses of escape
Which herd the plain in a mass unspoken poem.

Finally, they cease to hate: for although hate
Bursts from the air and whips the earth like hail
Or pours it up in fountains to marvel at,
And although hundreds fell, who can connect
The inexhaustible anger of the guns
With the dumb patience of these tormented animals?

Clean silence drops at night when a little walk
Divides the sleeping armies, each
Huddled in linen woven by remote hands.
When the machines are stilled, a common suffering
Whitens the air with breath and makes both one
As though these enemies slept in each other's arms.

Only the lucid friend to aerial raiders,
The brilliant pilot moon, stares down
Upon the plain she makes a shining bone
Cut by the shadow of many thousand bones.
Where amber clouds scatter on no-man's-land
She regards death and time throw up
The furious words and minerals which kill life.

c. 1939   STEPHEN SPENDER

To Margot Heinemann

Heart of the heartless world,
Dear heart, the thought of you
Is the pain at my side,
The shadow that chills my view.

The wind rises in the evening,
Reminds that autumn is near.
I am afraid to lose you,
I am afraid of my fear.

On the last mile to Huesca,
The last fence for our pride,
Think so kindly, dear, that I
Sense you at my side.

And if bad luck should lay my strength
Into the shallow grave,
Remember all the good you can;
Don't forget my love.

w. 1936   JOHN CORNFORD

Port Bou

As a child holds a pet
Arms clutching but with hands that do not join
And the coiled animal watches the gap
To outer freedom in animal air,
So the earth-and-rock flesh arms of this harbour
Embrace but do not enclose the sea
Which, through a gap, vibrates to the open sea

Where ships and dolphins swim and above is the sun.
In the bright winter sunlight I sit on the stone parapet
Of a bridge; my circling arms rest on a newspaper
Empty in my mind as the glittering stone
Because I search for an image
And seeing an image I count out the coined words
To remember the childish headlands of this harbour.
A lorry halts beside me with creaking brakes
And I look up at warm waving flag-like faces
Of militiamen staring down at my French newspaper.
'How do they speak of our struggle, over the frontier?'
I hold out the paper, but they refuse,
They did not ask for anything so precious
But only for friendly words and to offer me cigarettes.
In their smiling faces the war finds peace, the famished
    mouths
Of the rusty carbines brush against their trousers
Almost as fragilely as reeds;
And wrapped in a cloth – old mother in a shawl –
The terrible machine-gun rests.
They shout, salute back as the truck jerks forward
Over the vigorous hill, beyond the headland.
An old man passes, his running mouth,
With three teeth like bullets, spits out 'pom-pom-pom'.
The children run after; and, more slowly, the women
Clutching their clothes, follow over the hill;
Till the village is empty, for the firing practice,
And I am left alone on the bridge at the exact centre
Where the cleaving river trickles like saliva.
At the exact centre, solitary as a target,
Where nothing moves against a background of cardboard
    houses
Except the disgraceful skirring dogs; and the firing begins,
Across the harbour mouth from headland to headland
White flecks of foam gashed by lead in the sea;
And the echo trails over its iron lash

Whipping the flanks of the surrounding hills.
My circling arms rest on the newspaper,
My mind seems paper where dust and ink fall,
I tell myself the shooting is only for practice,
And my body seems a cloth which the machine-gun stitches
Like a sewing machine, neatly, with cotton from a reel;
And the solitary, irregular, thin 'paffs' from the carbines
Draw on long needles white threads through my navel.

c. 1939   STEPHEN SPENDER

Ultima Ratio Regum

The guns spell money's ultimate reason
In letters of lead on the spring hillside.
But the boy lying dead under the olive trees
Was too young and too silly
To have been notable to their important eye.
He was a better target for a kiss.

When he lived, tall factory hooters never summoned him.
Nor did restaurant plate-glass doors revolve to wave him in.
His name never appeared in the papers.
The world maintained its traditional wall
Round the dead with their gold sunk deep as a well,
Whilst his life, intangible as a Stock Exchange
            rumour, drifted outside.

O too lightly he threw down his cap
One day when the breeze threw petals from the trees.
The unflowering wall sprouted with guns,
Machine-gun anger quickly scythed the grasses;
Flags and leaves fell from hands and branches;
The tweed cap rotted in the nettles.

Consider his life which was valueless
In terms of employment, hotel ledgers, news files.
Consider. One bullet in ten thousand kills a man.
Ask. Was so much expenditure justified
On the death of one so young and so silly
Lying under the olive trees, O world, O death?

c. 1939   STEPHEN SPENDER

A Moment of War

It is night like a red rag
drawn across the eyes,

the flesh is bitterly pinned
to desperate vigilance,

the blood is stuttering with fear.

O praise the security of worms
and cool crumbs of soil,
flatter the hidden sap
and the lost unfertilized spawn of fish!

The hands melt with weakness
into the gun's hot iron,

the body melts with pity,

the face is braced for wounds,
the odour and the kiss of final pain.

O envy the peace of women
giving birth and love like toys
into the hands of men!

the mouth festers with pale curses,

the bowels struggle like a nest of rats,

the feet wish they were grass
spaced quietly.

O Christ and Mother!

But darkness opens like a knife for you
and you are marked down by your pulsing brain

and isolated,

and your breathing,

your breathing is the blast, the bullet,
and the final sky.

Montpellier   LAURIE LEE
  October 1937

Thoughts During an Air Raid

Of course, the entire effort is to put myself
Outside the ordinary range
Of what are called statistics. A hundred are killed
In the outer suburbs. Well, well, I carry on.
So long as the great 'I' is propped upon
This girdered bed which seems more like a hearse,
In the hotel bedroom with flowering wallpaper
Which rings in wreathes above, I can ignore
The pressure of those names under my fingers
Heavy and black as I rustle the paper,
The wireless wail in the lounge margin.
Yet supposing that a bomb should dive
Its nose right through this bed, with me upon it?
The thought is obscene. Still, there are many
To whom my death would only be a name,
One figure in a column. The essential is

That all the 'I's should remain separate
Propped up under flowers, and no one suffer
For his neighbour. Then horror is postponed
For everyone until it settles on him
And drags him to that incommunicable grief
Which is all mystery or nothing.

c. 1939   STEPHEN SPENDER

A Letter from Aragon

This is a quiet sector of a quiet front.

We buried Ruiz in a new pine coffin,
But the shroud was too small and his washed feet stuck out.
The stink of his corpse came through the clean pine boards
And some of the bearers wrapped handkerchiefs round their
    faces.
Death was not dignified.
We hacked a ragged grave in the unfriendly earth
And fired a ragged volley over the grave.

You could tell from our listlessness, no one much missed
    him.

This is a quiet sector of a quiet front.
There is no poison gas and no H.E.

But when they shelled the other end of the village
And the streets were choked with dust
Women came screaming out of the crumbling houses,
Clutched under one arm the naked rump of an infant.
I thought: how ugly fear is.

This is a quiet sector of a quiet front.
Our nerves are steady; we all sleep soundly.

In the clean hospital bed my eyes were so heavy
Sleep easily blotted out one ugly picture,
A wounded militiaman moaning on a stretcher,
Now out of danger, but still crying for water,
Strong against death, but unprepared for such pain.

This on a quiet front.

But when I shook hands to leave, an Anarchist worker
Said: 'Tell the workers of England
This was a war not of our own making,
We did not seek it.
But if ever the Fascists again rule Barcelona
It will be as a heap of ruins with us workers beneath it.'

w. 1936   JOHN CORNFORD

Music in a Spanish Town

In the street I take my stand
with my fiddle like a gun against my shoulder,
and the hot strings under my trigger hand
shooting an old dance at the evening walls.

Each salt-white house is a numbered tomb
its silent window crossed with blood;
my notes explode everywhere like bombs
when I should whisper in fear of the dead.

So my fingers falter, and run in the sun
like the limbs of a bird that is slain,
as my music searches the street in vain.

Suddenly there is a quick flutter of feet
and children crowd about me,
listening with sores and infected ears,
watching with lovely eyes and vacant lips.

Cordoba, 1936   LAURIE LEE

Words Asleep

Now I am still and spent
and lie in a whited sepulchre
breathing dead

but there will be
no lifting of the damp swathes
no return of blood
no rolling away the stone

till the cocks carve sharp
gild scars in the morning
and carry the stirring sun
and the early dust to my ears.

Andalucía, 1936   LAURIE LEE

The Hand that Signed the Paper

The hand that signed the paper felled a city;
Five sovereign fingers taxed the breath,
Doubled the globe of dead and halved a country;
These five kings did a king to death.

The mighty hand leads to a sloping shoulder,
The finger joints are cramped with chalk;
A goose's quill has put an end to murder
That put an end to talk.

The hand that signed the treaty bred a fever,
And famine grew, and locusts came;
Great is the hand that holds dominion over
Man by a scribbled name.

The five kings count the dead but do not soften
The crusted wounds nor pat the brow;
A hand rules pity as a hand rules heaven;
Hands have no tears to flow.

p. 1935   DYLAN THOMAS

Fall of a City

All the posters on the walls
All the leaflets in the streets
Are mutilated, destroyed or run in rain,
Their words blotted out with tears,
Skins peeling from their bodies
In the victorious hurricane.

All the names of heroes in the hall
Where the feet thundered and the bronze throats roared,
FOX and LORCA claimed as history on the walls,
Are now angrily deleted
Or to dust surrender their dust,
From golden praise excluded.

All the badges and salutes
Torn from lapels and from hands
Are thrown away with human sacks they wore

154

Or in the deepest bed of mind
They are washed over with a smile
Which launches the victors when they win.

All the lessons learned, unlearnt;
The young, who learned to read, now blind
Their eyes with an archaic film;
The peasant relapses to a stumbling tune
Following the donkey's bray;
These only remember to forget.

But somewhere some word presses
On the high door of a skull, and in some corner
Of an irrefrangible eye
Some old man's memory jumps to a child
– Spark from the days of energy.
And the child hoards it like a bitter toy.

c. 1939   STEPHEN SPENDER

Elegy on Spain

Dedication to the photograph of a child
killed in an air raid on Barcelona

O ecstatic is this head of five-year joy –
Captured its butterfly rapture on a paper:
And not the rupture of the right eye may
Make any less this prettier than a picture.
O now, my minor moon, dead as meat
Slapped on a negative plate, I hold
The crime of the bloody time in my hand.

Light, light with that lunar death our fate;
Make more dazzling with your agony's gold
The death that lays us all in the sand.

Gaze with that gutted eye on our endeavour
To be the human brute, not the brute human:
And if I feel your gaze upon me ever,
I'll wear the robe of blood that love illumines.

I

The hero's red rag is laid across his eyes,
Lies by the Madrid rock and baptizes sand
Grander than god with the blood of his best, and
Estramadura is blazing in his fallen hand.
All of a fallen man is what is heaven's;
Grievance is lowered to a half-mast of sorrow,
Tomorrow has no hand in the beat of his breath, and after
Laughter his heart is hollow.

For a star is against him, that fallen on his forehead,
Forward is blocked by the augury of our evil.
Sin is a star that has fallen on our own heads.
Sheds us a shower of chlorine, the devil's revel;
Evil lifts a hand and the heads of flowers fall –
The pall of the hero who by the Ebro bleeding
Feeds with his blood the stones that rise and call,
Tall as any man, 'No pasaran!'

Can the bird cry any other word on the branch
That blanches at the bomb's red wink and roar,
Or the tall daffodil, trodden under the wheel of war,
But spring up again in the Spring for will not stay under?
Thunder and Mussolini cannot forbid to sing and spring
The bird with a word of determination, or a blossom of hope.
Heard in a dream, or blooming down Time's slope.

But now for a moment which shall always be a moment
Draw like a murder the red rag across those eyes.
Skies in July not drier than they are,

Bare of a tear now that pain, like a crystal memorial,
Is their memorial scattered over the face of Spain.
Together this hero and the ghost of the Easter Irish,
Brother and sister, beaten by the fist of the beast,
Water tomorrow with the tears and blood of slaughter.

2

Go down, my red bull, proud as a hero,
Nero is done with, but the Hungerford Hundred,
The Tolpuddle Martyr, the human hero,
Rises and remains, not in loss sundered;
Plundered, is proud of his plenitude of prizes.
Now spiked with false friendship, bright with blood,
Stood did my bull in the pool of his passion,
Flashing his sickle horn as he sinks at the knees.

Peace is not angels blessing blood with a kiss; —
Is the axis pinning Spain through the breast
To the water-wheel that makes a nation a martyr
To the traitor who wheels the whips of gold and steel.
O bold bull in the ring, old ox at the wheel,
Sold for a song on the lips of a Hitler,
No halter shall hold you down to the bloody altar
Longer than life takes to rise again from slaughter.

This flower Freedom needs blood at the roots,
Its shoots spring from your wounds, and the bomb
Booming among the ruins of your houses, arouses
Generation and generation from the grave
To slave at your side for future liberation.
Those who die with five stars in their hands
Hand on their ghosts to guard a yard of land
From the boot of the landlord and the band of war.

Drop, drop that heavy head, my less and more than dead,
Bled dry a moment, tomorrow will raise that hand
From the sad sand, less than death a defeat
Beaten by friend, not enemy, betrayed, not beaten,
Laid let that head be, low, my bull, stunned,
Gunned from the royal box by a trigger pull.
Bigger no courage is than the blood it can spill.

Not in a wreath I write the death in a ring,
But sing a breath taken by heroes, a respite:
No fight is over when Satan still straddles a man;
Then the real battle begins which only ends
When friends shake hands over the break of evil.
O level out the outrageous crags of hate
To those great valleys where our love can slant
Like light at morning that restores the plant!

O Asturian with a burst breast like an aster,
Disaster sports blooms like that in many places;
Graces the grave of a nation with human pain.
Spain like a sleeping beauty finds her kiss
Is the lips of your wounds awakening her again
To claim her freedom from the enclosing chain.
Silence the blackbird, take away the tree,
He will not need them until he is free.

At evening is red the sky over us all.
Shall our fiery funeral not raise tomorrow also?
So shall the order of love from death's disorder
Broader than Russia arise and bring in the day.
Sleep gives us dreams that the morning dissolves,
But borne on death we reach the bourne of dreams.
Seems blood too bitter a bargain to pay for that day?
Too bitter a bargain, or too far a day?

Draw then the red sky over his eyes, and Sleep
Keep Orion silent above him, and no wind move
Love's leaves covering him at the French border.
The marauder snuffles among his guts for a night:
Right is capsized: but Spain shall not drown,
For grown to a giantess overnight arises,
Blazes like morning Venus on a bleeding sea,
She, he, shall stretch her limbs in liberty.

3

Madrid, like a live eye in the Iberian mask,
Asks help from heaven and receives a bomb:
Doom makes the night her eyelid, but at dawn
Drawn is the screen from the bull's-eye capital.
She gazes at the Junker angels in the sky
Passionately and pitifully. Die
The death of the dog. O Capital City, still
Sirius shall spring up from the kill.

Farewell for a day my phœnix who leaves ashes
Flashing on the Guernica tree and Guadalajara range.
Change is the ringing of all bells of evil,
Good is a constant that now lies in your keeping
Sleeping in the cemeteries of the fallen, who,
True as a circling star will soon return
Burning the dark with five tails of anger.

What is there not in the air any longer,
Stronger than songs or roses, and greater
Than those who create it, a nation
Manhandling god for its freedom? lost,
O my ghost, the first fall, but not lost
The will to liberty which shall have liberty
At the long last.

So close a moment that long open eye,
Fly the flag low, and fold over those hands
Cramped to a gun: gather the child's remains
Staining the wall and cluttering the drains;
Troop down the red to the black and the brown;
Go homeward with tears to water the ground.
All this builds a bigger plinth for glory,
Story on story, on which triumph shall be found.

p. 1939   GEORGE BARKER

Autumn Journal

VI

And I remember Spain
   At Easter ripe as an egg for revolt and ruin
Though for a tripper the rain
   Was worse than the surly or the worried or the haunted
      faces
With writings on the walls –
   Hammer and sickle, Boicot, Viva, Muerra;
With café au lait brimming the waterfalls,
   With sherry, shellfish, omelettes.
With fretted stone the Moor
   Had chiselled for effects of sun and shadow;
With shadows of the poor,
   The begging cripples and the children begging.
The churches full of saints
   Tortured on racks of marble –
The old complaints
   Covered with gilt and dimly lit with candles.
With powerful or banal
   Monuments of riches or repression
And the Escorial

Cold for ever within like the heart of Philip.
With ranks of dominoes
  Deployed on café tables the whole of Sunday
With cabarets that call the tourist, shows
  Of thighs and eyes and nipples.
With slovenly soldiers, nuns,
  And peeling posters from the last elections
Promising bread or guns
  Or an amnesty or another
Order or else the old
  Glory veneered and varnished
As if veneer could hold
  The rotten guts and crumbled bones together.
And a vulture hung in air
  Below the cliffs of Ronda and below him
His hook-winged shadow wavered like despair
  Across the chequered vineyards.
And the boot-blacks in Madrid
  Kept us half an hour with polish and pincers
And all we did
  In that city was drink and think and loiter.
And in the Prado half-
  wit princes looked from the canvas they had paid for
(Goya had the laugh –
  But can what is corrupt be cured by laughter?)
And the day at Aranjuez
  When the sun came out for once on the yellow river
With Valdepeñas burdening the breath
  We slept a royal sleep in the royal gardens;
And at Toledo walked
  Around the ramparts where they throw the garbage
And glibly talked
  Of how the Spaniards lack all sense of business.
And Avila was cold
  And Segovia was picturesque and smelly
And a goat on the road seemed old

As the rocks or the Roman arches.
And Easter was wet and full
  In Seville and in the ring on Easter Sunday
A clumsy bull and then a clumsy bull
  Nodding his banderillas died of boredom.
And the standard of living was low
  But that, we thought to ourselves, was not our business;
All that the tripper wants is the *status quo*
  Cut and dried for trippers.
And we thought the papers a lark
  With their party politics and blank invective;
And we thought the dark
  Women who dyed their hair should have it dyed more
    often.
And we sat in trains all night
  With the windows shut among civil guards and peasants
And tried to play piquet by a tiny light
  And tried to sleep bolt upright;
And cursed the Spanish rain
  And cursed their cigarettes which came to pieces
And caught heavy colds in Cordova and in vain
  Waited for the right light for taking photos.
And we met a Cambridge don who said with an air
  'There's going to be trouble shortly in this country',
And ordered anis, pudgy and debonair,
  Glad to show off his mastery of the language.
But only an inch behind
  This map of olive and ilex, this painted hoarding,
Careless of visitors the people's mind
  Was tunnelling like a mole to day and danger.
And the day before we left
  We saw the mob in flower at Algeciras
Outside a toothless door, a church bereft
  Of its images and its aura.
And at La Linea while
  The night put miles between us and Gibraltar

We heard the blood-lust of a drunkard pile
  His heaven high with curses;
And next day took the boat
  For home, forgetting Spain, not realizing
That Spain would soon denote
  Our grief, our aspirations;
Not knowing that our blunt
  Ideals would find their whetstones, that our spirit
Would find its frontier on the Spanish front,
  Its body in a rag-tag army.

c. 1939   LOUIS MACNEICE

V. AS FOR OURSELVES

To a Writer on His Birthday

August for the people and their favourite islands.
Daily the steamers sidle up to meet
The effusive welcome of the pier, and soon
The luxuriant life of the steep stone valleys
The sallow oval faces of the city
Begot in passion or good-natured habit
Are caught by waiting coaches, or laid bare
Beside the undiscriminating sea.

Lulled by the light they live their dreams of freedom,
May climb the old road twisting to the moors,
Play leapfrog, enter cafés, wear
The tigerish blazer and the dove-like shoe.
The yachts upon the little lake are theirs,
The gulls ask for them, and to them the band
Makes its tremendous statements; they control
The complicated apparatus of amusement.

All types that can intrigue the writer's fancy
Or sensuality approves are here.
And I each meal-time with the families
The animal brother and his serious sister,
Or after breakfast on the urned steps watching
The defeated and disfigured marching by,
Have thought of you, Christopher, and wished beside me
Your squat spruce body and enormous head.

Nine years ago upon that southern island
Where the wild Tennyson became a fossil,
Half-boys, we spoke of books, and praised
The acid and austere, behind us only
The stuccoed suburb and expensive school.

Scented our turf, the distant baying
Nice decoration to the artist's wish.
Yet fast the deer was flying through the wood.

Our hopes were set still on the spies' career,
Prizing the glasses and the old felt hat,
And all the secrets we discovered were
Extraordinary and false; for this one coughed
And it was gasworks coke, and that one laughed
And it was snow in bedrooms; many wore wigs,
The coastguard signalled messages of love,
The enemy were sighted from the norman tower.

Five summers pass and now we watch
The Baltic from a balcony: the word is love.
Surely one fearless kiss would cure
The million fevers, a stroking brush
The insensitive refuse from the burning core.
Was there a dragon who had closed the works
While the starved city fed it with the Jews?
Then love would tame it with his trainer's look.

Pardon the studied taste that could refuse
The golf-house quick one and the rector's tea;
Pardon the nerves the thrushes could not soothe,
Yet answered promptly the no-subtler lure
To private joking in a panelled room.
The solitary vitality of tramps and madmen,
Believed the whisper in the double bed.
Pardon for these and every flabby fancy.

For now the moulding images of growth
That made our interest and us, are gone.
Louder today the wireless roars
Its warnings and its lies, and it's impossible
Among the well-shaped cosily to flit,

Or longer to desire about our lives
The beautiful loneliness of the banks, or find
The stores and resignations of the frozen plains.

The close-set eyes of mother's boy
Saw nothing to be done; we look again
See scandal praying with her sharp knees up
And virtue stood at Weeping Cross
And Courage to his leaking ship appointed,
Slim Truth dismissed without a character
And gaga Falsehood highly recommended,
The green thumb to the ledger knuckled down.

Greed showing shamelessly her naked money
And all love's wandering eloquence debased
To a collector's slang. Smartness in furs
And Beauty scratching miserably for food,
Honour self-sacrificed for Calculation
And reason stoned by mediocrity,
Freedom by power shamefully maltreated
And Justice exiled till Saint Geoffrey's Day.

So in this hour of crisis and dismay
What better than your strict and adult pen
Can warn us from the colours and the consolations,
The showy arid works, reveal
The squalid shadow of academy and garden,
Make action urgent and its nature clear?
Who give us nearer insight to resist
The expanding fear, the savaging disaster?

This then my birthday wish for you, as now
From the narrow window of my fourth floor room
I smoke into the night, and watch reflections
Stretch in the harbour. In the houses
The little pianos are closed, and a clock strikes.

And all sway forward on the dangerous flood
Of history that never sleeps or dies,
And, held one moment, burns the hand.

p. 1935   W. H. AUDEN

Autumn Journal

XV

Shelley and jazz and lieder and love and hymn-tunes
  And day returns too soon;
We'll get drunk among the roses
  In the valley of the moon.
Give me an aphrodisiac, give me lotus,
  Give me the same again;
Make all the erotic poets of Rome and Ionia
  And Florence and Provence and Spain
Pay a tithe of their sugar to my potion
  And ferment my days
With the twang of Hawaii and the boom of the Congo;
  Let the old Muse loosen her stays
Or give me a new Muse with stockings and suspenders
  And a smile like a cat,
With false eyelashes and finger-nails of carmine
  And dressed by Schiaparelli, with a pill-box hat.
Let the aces run riot round Brooklands,
  Let the tape-machines go drunk,
Turn on the purple spotlight, pull out the Vox Humana,
  Dig up somebody's body in a cloakroom trunk.
Give us sensations and then again sensations –
  Strip-tease, fireworks, all-in wrestling, gin;
Spend your capital, open your house and pawn your
    padlocks,
  Let the critical sense go out and the Roaring Boys
    come in.

Give me a houri but houris are too easy,
 Give me a nun;
We'll rape the angels off the golden reredos
 Before we're done.
Tiger-women and Lesbos, drums and entrails,
 And let the skies rotate,
We'll play roulette with the stars, we'll sit out drinking
 At the Hangman's Gate.
O look who comes here. I cannot see their faces
 Walking in file, slowly in file;
They have no shoes on their feet, the knobs of their ankles
 Catch the moonlight as they pass the stile
And cross the moor among the skeletons of bog-oak
 Following the track from the gallows back to the town;
Each has the end of a rope around his neck. I wonder
 Who let these men come back, who cut them down –
And now they reach the gate and line up opposite
 The neon lights on the medieval wall
And underneath the sky-signs
 Each one takes his cowl and lets it fall
And we see their faces, each the same as the other,
 Men and women, each like a closed door,
But something about their faces is familiar;
 Where have we seen them before?
Was it the murderer on the nursery ceiling
 Or Judas Iscariot in the Field of Blood
Or someone at Gallipoli or in Flanders
 Caught in the end-all mud?
But take no notice of them, out with the ukelele,
 The saxophone and the dice;
They are sure to go away if we take no notice;
 Another round of drinks or make it twice.
That was a good one, tell us another, don't stop talking,
 Cap your stories; if
You haven't any new ones tell the old ones,

Tell them as often as you like and perhaps those horrible
   stiff
People with blank faces that are yet familiar
   Won't be there when you look again, but don't
Look just yet, just give them time to vanish. I said to vanish;
   What do you mean – they won't?
Give us the songs of Harlem or Mitylene –
   Pearls in wine –
There can't be a hell unless there is a heaven
   And a devil would have to be divine
And there can't be such things one way or the other;
   That we know;
You can't step into the same river twice so there can't be
   Ghosts; thank God that rivers always flow.
Sufficient to the moment is the moment;
   Past and future merely don't make sense
And yet I thought I had seen them . . .
   But *how*, if there is only a present tense?
Come on, boys, we aren't afraid of bogies,
   Give us another drink;
This little lady has a fetish,
   She goes to bed in mink.
This little pig went to market –
   Now I think you may look, I think the coast is clear.
Well, why don't you answer?
   I can't answer because they are still there.

c. 1939   LOUIS MACNEICE

Distant View of a Provincial Town

Beside those spires so spick and span
   Against an unencumbered sky
The old Great Western Railway ran
   When someone different was I.

St Aidan's with the prickly nobs
   And iron spikes and coloured tiles –
Where Auntie Maud devoutly bobs
   In those enriched vermilion aisles:

St George's where the mattins bell
   But rarely drowned the trams for prayer –
No Popish sight or sound or smell
   Disturbed that gas-invaded air:

St Mary's where the Rector preached
   In such a jolly friendly way
On cricket, football, things that reached
   The simple life of every day:

And that United Benefice
   With entrance permanently locked, –
How Gothic, grey and sad it is
   Since Mr Grogley was unfrocked!

The old Great Western Railway shakes
   The old Great Western Railway spins –
The old Great Western Railway makes
   Me very sorry for my sins.

c. 1937   JOHN BETJEMAN

Forgive me, Sire

Forgive me, sire, for cheating your intent,
That I, who should command a regiment,
Do amble amiably here, O God,
One of the neat ones in your awkward squad.

p. 1935   NORMAN CAMERON

Lament for a Lost Life

What shall I do the long, long day?
  O, where shall I find a lover?
Will no one come to drive me away,
  A prince or a rover?

I know there are moors where huntsmen ride
  From their white expensive houses;
And yachts that lovingly wait the tide,
  Or the wind arouses.

I know there are gowns as lovely as snow
  In shops I cannot enter;
And furs, O softer than love, for show
  But not for wear this winter.

I know there are beautiful open drives
  Where leisurely cars are waiting:
O, why out of all these fortunate lives
  Should I be found wanting?

Will the Rolls draw up at my careless door?
  Will the neighbours stand and admire?
Shall we speed away to a foreign shore,
  Shall I have my desire?

For O there is music more thrilling than wine
  Comes whispering over the sea:
In his confident arms the world shall be mine
  And Time just eternity.

Let the clock tick its anguishing seconds,
  Time is no larger than passion at last:
And the kiss of my hero shall make amends
  For the snubs of the past.

In the casino the chatter will cease:
  The glamorous wonder and stare:
A mysterious lady: and who shall guess
  How beautiful and rare?

Easy to lose an enormous sum,
  More than anyone ever won:
Silence the self-assured and numb
  The room when I've gone.

Royal babies should be praised much less
  Than my adoring twins:
Sunday papers lavishly will stress
  My extravagant sins.

Gowns and silks to wear for an hour,
  Jewels that freeze the heart:
Scent that has the fragrance and the power
  To surrender and hurt.

O, what shall I do the long, long day
  But dream of what never will be.
The husband and neighbours have gone away,
  Nobody comes at three.

There's nothing to fill an engagement book:
  There's nowhere to take the car;
Not even the tradesmen seem to look
  At my eyes as they are.

Never the sea will flood this street,
  Or mountains spring from the road:
I'll never run lightly or gaily to meet
  One from my dream or a god.

O, what shall I do the long, long day?
   Where shall I find a lover?
Will no one come to take me away,
   Death or another?

p. 1939   H. B. MALLALIEU

Light and Air

1

Our private vision is death, and the seers are yellow
who saw something remarkable in the dark,
who left the gas turned on, but never lit it,
and innocently withdrew before the explosion,
only too glad to forgive everyone.

Broken fragments are left, pieces of pottery,
fragments of branch or frond for the microscope,
groups seen for an instant in indistinct light,
sometimes a curious smell outside the window.

We sometimes raise our heads from the window sill.
We sometimes venture to the ruinous door;
in the creaking house we demand light and air;

for what we need most is an atmosphere
fit to be breathed, and light by which to see.

2

The prisoner, or guest in an old house
uncertain of the stability of his room,
or traveller at night in an unknown ground,
or in the dark sea, clinging to cork, the sailor,
longs for the light, but most the prisoner.

All light, even the hot hand of the eastern sun
shredding the curtains, wood-blisterer, pursuer of bats;
even the python noon dragging over the sand,
or cascading blank streets with hawk's downpouring glare;

even the pale of pearl, nip, clip of dawn
on cold coasts curling over the grey waves,
dim icy glow through scurrying legs of waders;

even through chimney stacks, swaddled in smoke,
sunlight through the soot striving to reach each face.

3

Wind, shoveller of seas, shuffler of leaves, wind
swaying the creaking trunks, puffing the distracted sedge,
twirler of straws, high handler of reeling rooks,
scattering them in smoky cloud like ashes of burnt paper;

looser of leaves' luxury, laying a bed for spring,
marrer of miles of dead wood, fanner into fire,
heaven's hound, panting, overrunning the fugitive world;

let us begin to imagine how life blows
restless resistless round our shuttered shacks.

Listen to bang of shutters, whistle in the iron
of air aiming at lungs, running through rotten timbers,
rocking the roof, whistling a wintry air,
that we may make way for ruin and rebuild
houses to welcome air, ready for the light of spring.

C. 1937   REX WARNER

Suburban Cemetery

Memorial marble columns with partial pride
Identify the commonplace with a saint's epitaph:
Precise rows of surprised angels
Folding their postscript wings at impossible angles
Stand on perpetual parade
Marking each one a private compartment of death.

Nettles of neglect caressing plinthbound feet
Spring's faded flowers rotting in brackish water,
Mock yesterday's endless sorrow:
No splendid defiant decay of ancient barrow
Convex against fate;
Even the silence is tawdry like sawdust laughter.

See an old woman resistless against marble magnet
Back bent in daily posied pilgrimage
Dead twig in hand, removing
The sacrilegious lump of a dog's leaving.
Beneath her feet
Mouldering master merges with the place.

Shackled with conscious desire to sorrow's slab
Her relict body, assenting to motions of grief
Yields peppercorn penance,
Observing formal due to the smothered tenant
Her physical hub:
Absent mind's orbit revolves in a different groove.

When through rusted gates scrunches a new inmate
The indifferent dead are unaware of their brother.
Grey owners of living faces
Shoot their cuffs and assume appropriate grimaces
Wind to the vacant lot
Ending the carriage talk as they silently gather.

One, two or three pawn their hearts for a small price,
To be redeemed after a decent period has passed:
Others lost in dreams
Aware of brewery smell and clutter of trams
Slip death's embrace
Jangling their pockets with promise of bequest.

Easing fingers explore between flesh and unusual starch;
Luxurious tears make dough of scented powder;
All find relief in flowers
Pointing with pride to the ticketed wreath which is theirs:
Obscene intruder
Wind with invisible hand flutters the mourning skirts.

Conclusion comes without an end being reached.
Boxed ambassador to the doubtful future
Left to devouring earth
After digestion will find vegetable re-birth.
To a different feast
They briskly return past staring angels, composing their
features.

p. 1937   GEOFFREY PARSONS

An Epistle to a Patron

My lord, hearing lately of your opulence in promises and
    your house
Busy with parasites, of your hands full of favours, your
    statues
Admirable as music and no fear of your arms not prospering,
    I have
Considered how to serve you and breed from my talents
These few secrets which I shall make plain

179

To your intelligent glory. You should understand that I
  have plotted

Being in command of all the ordinary engines

Of defence and offence, a hundred and fifteen buildings

Less others less complete: complete, some are courts of
  serene stone

Some the civil structures of a war-like elegance as bridges

Sewers, aqueducts, and citadels of brick with which I
  declare the fact

That your nature is to vanquish. For these I have acquired
  a knowledge

Of the habits of numbers and of various tempers and skill in
  setting

Firm sets of pure bare members which will rise, hanging
  together

Like an argument, with beams, ties and sistering pilasters:

The lintels and windows with mouldings as round as a girl's
  chin; thresholds

To libraries; halls that cannot be entered without a sensa-
  tion as of myrrh

By your vermilion officers, your sages and dancers. There
  will be chambers

Like the recovery of a sick man, your closet waiting not

Less suitably shadowed than the heart, and the coffers of a
  ceiling

To reflect your diplomatic taciturnities. You may commis-
  sion

Hospitals, huge granaries that will smile to bear your filial
  plunders

And stables washed with a silver lime in whose middle tower
  seated

In the slight acridity you may watch

The copper thunder kept in the sulky flanks of your horse, a
  rolling field

Of necks glad to be groomed, the strong crupper, the edged
  hoof

And the long back, seductive and rebellious to saddles.

And barracks, fortresses in need of no vest save light, light

That to me is breath, food and drink, I live by effects of
 light, I live

To catch it, to break it, as an orator plays off

Against each other and his theme his casual gems, and so
 with light

Twisted in strings, plucked, crossed or knotted, or crumbled

As it may be allowed to be by leaves

Or clanged back by lakes and rocks or otherwise beaten

Or else split and spread like a feast of honey, dripping

Through delightful voids and creeping along long fractures,
 brimming

Carved canals, bowls and lachrymatories with pearls: All
 this the work

Of now advancing now withdrawing faces, whose use I
 know.

I know what slabs thus will be soaked to a thumb's depth by
 the sun

And where to rob them, what colour stifles in your intact
 quarries, what

Sand silted in your river-gorges will well mix with the dust
 of flint, I know

What wood to cut by what moon in what weather

Of your sea-winds, your hill-wind therefore tyrant, let me
 learn

Your high-ways, ways of sandstone, roads of the oakleaf and
 your sea-ways.

Send me to dig dry graves, exposing what you want. I must

Attend your orgies and debates (let others apply for austeri-
 ties) admit me

To your witty table, stuff me with urban levities, feed me,
 bind me

To a prudish luxury, free me thus and with a workshop

From my household consisting

Of a pregnant wife, one female and one boy child and an
elder bastard

With other properties, these let me regard, let me neglect
and let

What I begin be finished. Save me, noble sir, from the
agony

Of starved and privy explorations such as those I stumble

From a hot bed to make, to follow lines to which the night-
sky

Holds only faint contingencies. These flights with no end
but failure

And failure not to end them, these palliate or prevent.

I wish for liberty, let me then be tied. And seeing too much

I aspire to be constrained by your emblems of birth and
triumph

And between the obligations of your future and the checks
of actual state

To flourish, adapt the stubs of an interminable descent and
place

The crested key to confident vaults, with a placid flurry of
petals

And bosom and lips will stony functionaries support

The persuasion, so beyond proof, of your power. I will record

In peculiar scrolls your alien alliances

Fit an apartment for your eastern hostage, extol in basalt

Your father, praise with white festoons the goddess your
lady,

And for your death which will be mine prepare

An encasement as if of solid blood. And so let me

Forget, let me remember that this is stone, stick, metal, trash

Which I will pile and hack, my hands will stain and bend

(None better knowing how to gain from the slow pains of a
marble

Bruised, breathing strange climates). Being pressed as I am,
being broken

By wealth and poverty, torn between strength and weakness, take me, choose
To relieve me, to receive of me and must you not agree
As you have been to some – a great giver of banquets, of respite from swords
Who shook out figured clothes, who rained coin
A donor of laurel and of grapes, a font of profuse intoxicants and so
To be so too for me? And none too soon, since the panting mind
Rather than barren will be prostitute and once
I served a herd of merchants: but since I will be faithful
And my virtue is such, though far from home let what is yours be mine and this be a match
As many have been proved, enduring exiles and blazed
Not without issue in returning shows: your miserly freaks
Your envies, racks and poisons not out of mind
Although not told, since often borne – indeed how should it be
That you employed them less than we? but now be flattered a little
To indulge the extravagant gist of this communication.
For my pride puts all in doubt and at present I have no patience
I have simply hope and I submit me
To your judgement which will be just.

c. 1938   F. T. PRINCE

Evasions

How many times have you smiled a reckoning smile
Either when there was some question of money
Or to humour one of the dead who live around?
– Oh, but that's been going on since the world began.

How many times face to face with your lover
Have you housed apart contracted with fear and cunning
Hidden from the body and that violent weather?
– Oh but that's been going on since the fall of man.

How many times smelling the smell of poverty
Have you tried and turned for good to your cornfield and
 garden
(And cornfield and garden grew foul pods and rotted)?
– Oh but that's been going on since the world began.

p. 1935   BERNARD SPENCER

Reflection from Anita Loos

No man is sure he does not need to climb.
It is not human to feel safely placed.
'A girl can't go on laughing all the time.'

Wrecked by their games and jeering at their prime
There are who can, but who can praise their taste?
No man is sure he does not need to climb.

Love rules the world but is it rude, or slime?
All nasty things are sure to be disgraced.
A girl can't go on laughing all the time.

Christ stinks of torture who was caught in lime.
No star he aimed at is entirely waste.
No man is sure he does not need to climb.

It is too weak to speak of right and crime.
Gentlemen prefer bound feet and the wasp waist.
A girl can't go on laughing all the time.

It gives a million gambits for a mime
On which a social system can be based:
No man is sure he does not need to climb,
A girl can't go on laughing all the time.

c. 1940   WILLIAM EMPSON

I Have Longed to Move Away

I have longed to move away
From the hissing of the spent lie
And the old terror's continual cry
Growing more terrible as the day
Goes over the hill into the deep sea;
I have longed to move away
From the repetition of salutes,
For there are ghosts in the air
And ghostly echoes on paper,
And the thunder of calls and notes.

I have longed to move away but am afraid;
Some life, yet unspent, might explode
Out of the old lie burning on the ground,
And, cracking into the air, leave me half-blind.
Neither by night's ancient fear,
The parting of hat from hair,
Pursed lips at the receiver,
Shall I fall to death's feather.
By these I would not care to die,
Half convention and half lie.

p. 1935   DYLAN THOMAS

Resolution of Dependence

> We poets in our youth begin in gladness,
> But thereof come in the end despondency and madness.
> Wordsworth: 'Resolution and Independence'.

I encountered the crowd returning from amusements,
The Bournemouth Pavilion, or the marvellous gardens,
The Palace of Solace, the Empyrean Cinema; and saw
William Wordsworth was one, tawdrily conspicuous,
Obviously emulating the old man of the mountain-moor,
Traipsing along on the outskirts of the noisy crowd.

Remarkable I reflected that after all it is him.
The layers of time falling continuously on Grasmere Church-
    yard,
The accumulation of year and year like calendar,
The acute superstition that Wordsworth is after all dead,
Should have succeeded in keeping him quiet and cold.
I resent the resurrection when I feel the updraught of fear.

But approaching me with a watch in his hand, he said:
'I fear you are fairly early; I expected a man; I see that
Already your private rebellion has been quelled.
Where are the violent gestures of the individualist?
I observe the absence of the erratic, the strange;
Where is the tulip, the rose, or the bird in hand?'

I had the heart to relate the loss of my charms,
The paradise pets I kept in my pocket, the bird,
The tulip trumpet, the penis water pistol;
I had the heart to have mourned them, but no word.
'I have done little reading,' I murmured, 'I have
Most of the time been trying to find an equation.'

He glanced over my shoulder at the evening promenade.
The passing people, like St. Vitus, averted their eyes:
I saw his eyes like a bent pin searching for eyes
To grip and catch. 'It is a species,' he said,
'I feel I can hardly cope with – it is ghosts, .
Trailing, like snails, an excrement of blood.

'I have passed my hand like postman's into them;
The information I dropped in at once dropped out.'
'No,' I answered, 'they received your bouquet of daffodils –
They speak of your feeling for Nature even now.'
He glanced at his watch. I admired a face.
The town clock chimed like a cat in a well.

'Since the private rebellion, the personal turn,
Leads down to the river with the dead cat and dead dog,
Since the single act of protest like a foggy film
Looks like women bathing, the Irish Lakes, or St. Vitus,
Susceptible of innumerable interpretations,
I can only advise a suicide or a resolution.'

'I can resolve,' I answered, 'if you can absolve.
Relieve me of my absurd and abysmal past.'
'I cannot relieve or absolve – the only absolution
Is final resolution to fix on the facts.
I mean more and less than British and Death; I also mean
The mechanical paraphernalia in between.'

'Not you and not him, not me, but all of them.
It is the conspiracy of five hundred million
To keep alive and kick. This is the resolution,
To keep us alive and kicking with strength or joy.
The past's absolution is the present's resolution:
The equation is the interdependence of parts.'

p. 1937   GEORGE BARKER

The Pharos

Still we can see it, that glorious peak,
Even though night is come, and silence has
Lowered an equal hand on myriad sound.
Stand with me now before our tent, stress face
To the wind's boisterous kiss and feel with me
The strong invisible cables drawing
Our gaze toward the mountain, luminous
Gigantic needle brightly etching sky.

O my young comrade, does the current pull
Your way with mine? The summit's influence,
It's fluid gentle will, has reached two cores
And struck their actions' positive response.
Climbing and sighing, and no rest, is ours
Till at that haven stars drop down on us.

c. 1935   CLIFFORD DYMENT

Poem

If truth can still be told
In this, the biased word,
If courage to pursue
Inside an empty head
This dream, the false discoverer
Of a new Europe and Asia,
If truth then may I be
Embarked on this sea,

To sail the narrow straits,
Stop by the Fortunate Islands;
And find monotonous

The liars' dear beguiling;
Theré leave the happy sailors
Time-caught like flies in rock,
With the expected disaster,
The organized shock.

p. 1937   JULIAN SYMONS

Request for the Day

Lord O never let lose this habit
of expected strangeness, a kind
of alertness ambushed in the eye,
at once to strike on, to select
the deep the dangerous uniqueness down in things;

That usual sites, often repeated walks
be minutely discovered more extraordinary
than gunfire in the mountains,
or the inland appearance of a tern
tumbling and white in ragamuffin chase
with swallows about the sky.

These that at common corners await
our boys, eager as ash-plants with their lightning tread,
for motive influence and a prevailing grandeur,
more than cold texts can longer carry
or their monumental heroes stiffened in stone.

Whose tiptoe awareness, tautening vitality,
joy's detailed confirmation, makes him ready;
prepares the achieved estate, the spirit's full perception
unarmed for wonder, a man moving in love.

c. 1933   RANDALL SWINGLER

The Dream

Dear, though the night is gone,
The dream still haunts to-day,
That brought us to a room,
Cavernous, lofty as
A railway terminus;
And crowded in that gloom
Were beds, and we in one
In a far corner lay.

Our whisper woke no clocks,
We kissed, and I was glad
At everything you did,
Indifferent to those
Who sat with hostile eyes
In pairs on every bed,
Arms round each other's necks,
Inert and vaguely sad.

O but what worm of guilt
Or what malignant doubt
Am I the victim of?
That you then, unabashed,
Did what I never wished,
Confessed another love,
And I, submissive, felt
Unwanted and went out.

p. 1936

W. H. AUDEN

Lay Your Sleeping Head

Lay your sleeping head, my love,
Human on my faithless arm;
Time and fevers burn away
Individual beauty from
Thoughtful children, and the grave
Proves the child ephemeral:
But in my arms till break of day
Let the living creature lie,
Mortal, guilty, but to me
The entirely beautiful.

Soul and body have no bounds:
To lovers as they lie upon
Her tolerant enchanted slope
In their ordinary swoon,
Grave the vision Venus sends
Of supernatural sympathy,
Universal love and hope;
While an abstract insight wakes
Among the glaciers and the rocks
The hermit's sensual ecstasy.

Certainty, fidelity
On the stroke of midnight pass
Like vibrations of a bell,
And fashionable madmen raise
Their pedantic boring cry;
Every farthing of the cost
All the dreaded cards foretell
Shall be paid, but from this night
Not a whisper, not a thought,
Not a kiss nor look be lost.

Beauty, midnight, vision dies:
Let the winds of dawn that blow
Softly round your dreaming head
Such a day of sweetness show
Eye and knocking heart may bless,
Find the mortal world enough;
Noons of dryness see you fed
By the involuntary powers,
Nights of insult let you pass
Watched by every human love.

p. 1937   W. H. AUDEN

Meeting Point

Time was away and somewhere else,
There were two glasses and two chairs
And two people with the one pulse
(Somebody stopped the moving stairs):
Time was away and somewhere else.

And they were neither up nor down,
The stream's music did not stop
Flowing through heather, limpid brown,
Although they sat in a coffee shop
And they were neither up nor down.

The bell was silent in the air
Holding its inverted poise –
Between the clang and clang a flower,
A brazen calyx of no noise:
The bell was silent in the air.

The camels crossed the miles of sand
That stretched around the cups and plates;

The desert was their own, they planned
To portion out the stars and dates:
The camels crossed the miles of sand.

Time was away and somewhere else.
The waiter did not come, the clock
Forgot them and the radio waltz
Came out like water from a rock:
Time was away and somewhere else.

Her fingers flicked away the ash
That bloomed again in tropic trees:
Not caring if the markets crash
When they had forests such as these,
Her fingers flicked away the ash.

God or whatever means the Good
Be praised that time can stop like this,
That what the heart has understood
Can verify in the body's peace
God or whatever means the Good.

Time was away and she was here
And life no longer what it was,
The bell was silent in the air
And all the room a glow because
Time was away and she was here.

April 1939   LOUIS MACNEICE

To a Greedy Lover

What is this recompense you'd have from me?
Melville asked no compassion of the sea.
Roll to and fro, forgotten in my wrack,
Love as you please – I owe you nothing back.

p. 1936   NORMAN CAMERON

In the Queen's Room

In smoky outhouses of the court of love
I chattered, a recalcitrant underling
Living on scraps. 'Below stairs or above,'
'All's one,' I said. 'We valets have our fling.'

Now I am come, by a chance beyond reach,
Into your room, my body smoky and soiled
And on my lips the taint of chattering speech,
Tell me, queen, am I irretrievably spoiled?

p. 1936   NORMAN CAMERON

Aubade

Hours before dawn we were woken by the quake.
My house was on a cliff. The thing could take
Bookloads off shelves, break bottles in a row.
Then the long pause and then the bigger shake.
It seemed the best thing to be up and go.

And far too large for my feet to step by.
I hoped that various buildings were brought low.
The heart of standing is you cannot fly.

It seemed quite safe till she got up and dressed.
The guarded tourist makes the guide the test.
Then I said The Garden? Laughing she said No.
Taxi for her and for me healthy rest.
It seemed the best thing to be up and go.

The language problem but you have to try.
Some solid ground for lying could she show?
The heart of standing is you cannot fly.

None of these deaths were her point at all.
The thing was that being woken he would bawl
And finding her not in earshot he would know.
I tried saying Half an Hour to pay this call.
It seemed the best thing to be up and go.

I slept, and blank as that I would yet lie.
Till you have seen what a threat holds below,
The heart of standing is you cannot fly.

Tell me again about Europe and her pains,
Who's tortured by the drought, who by the rains.
Glut me with floods where only the swine can row
Who cuts his throat and let him count his gains.
It seemed the best thing to be up and go.

A bedshift flight to a Far Eastern sky.
Only the same war on a stronger toe.
The heart of standing is you cannot fly.

Tell me more quickly what I lost by this,
Or tell me with less drama what they miss
Who call no die a god for a good throw,
Who says after two aliens had one kiss
It seemed the best thing to be up and go.

But as to risings, I can tell you why.
It is on contradiction that they grow.
It seemed the best thing to be up and go.
Up was the heartening and the strong reply.
The heart of standing is we cannot fly.

c. 1940   WILLIAM EMPSON

Elegy on the Heroine of Childhood
(in memory of Pearl White)

'. . . We died in you, and offered
Sweets to the Gods . . .'

Who flung this world? What gangs proclaimed a truce,
Spinning the streets from bootlaces come loose?
What iron·hoop in darkness slid
Chased by electric heels which hid
Cold faces behind pamphlets of the time?
Why was I left? What stairs had I to climb?

Four words catch hold. Dead exile, you would excite
In the red darkness, through the filtered light,
Our round, terrified eyes, when some
Demon of the rocks would come
And lock you in his house of moving walls:
You taught us first how loudly a pin falls.

From penny rows, when we began to spell,
We watched you, at the time when Arras fell,
Saw you, as in a death-ray seen,
Ride the real fear on a propped screen,
Where, through revolting brass, and darkness' bands,
Gaping, we groped with unawakened hands.

A sea-swung murmur, and a shout. Like shags
Under carved gods, with sweets in cone-shaped bags,
Tucked in tomorrow's unpaid fears,
Rucked there before the unguarded years,
We watched you, doomed, drowned, daggered, hurled
    from sight,
Fade from your clipped death in the tottering light.

Frantic, a blunted pattern showed you freed.
Week back to week I tread with nightmare speed,
Find the small entrance to large days,
Charging the chocolates from the trays,
Where, trailing or climbing the railing, we mobbed the dark
Of Pandemonium near Cwmdonkin Park.

Children return to mourn you. I retrace
Their steps to childhood's jealousies, a place
Of urchin hatred, shaken fists;
I drink the poison of the mists
To see you, a clear ghost before true day,
A girl, through wrestling clothes, caps flung in play.

From school's spiked railings, glass-topped, cat-walked walls,
From albums strewn, the streets' strange funerals,
We run to join the queue's coiled peel
Tapering, storming the Bastille,
Tumbling, with collars torn and scattered ties,
To thumbscrewed terror and the sea of eyes.

Night falls. The railing on which fast we pressed
Bears you, thumb-printed, to a death unguessed,
Before the time when you should rise
Venus to adolescent eyes,
A mermaid drying from your acid bath
Catching our lechery on a flying path.

Who has not seen the falling of a star?
Black liquorice made you bright before the War.
You glittered where the tongue was curled
Around the sweet fear of this world.
Doom's serial writing sprang upon the wall
Blind with a rush of light. We saw you fall.

How near, how far, how very faintly comes
Your tempest through a tambourine of crumbs,
Whose eye by darkness sanctified,
Is brilliant with my boyhood's slide.
How silently at last the reel runs back
Through your three hundred deaths, now Death wears
    black.

w. 1939   VERNON WATKINS

This Last Pain

This last pain for the damned the Fathers found:
'They knew the bliss with which they were not crowned.'
    Such, but on earth, let me foretell,
    Is all, of heaven or of hell.

Man, as the prying housemaid of the soul,
May know her happiness by eye to hole:
    He's safe; the key is lost; he knows
    Door will not open, nor hole close.

'What is conceivable can happen too,'
Said Wittgenstein, who had dreamt of you;
    But wisely; if we worked it long
    We should forget where it was wrong.

Those thorns being crowns which, woven into knots,
Crackle under and soon boil fool's pots;
    And no man's watching, wise and long,
    Would ever stare them into song.

All those large dreams by which men long live well
Are magic-lanterned on the smoke of hell;
    This then is real, I have implied,
    A painted, small, transparent slide.

These the inventive can hand-paint at leisure,
Or all emporia would stock our measure;
  And feasting in their dappled shade
  We should forget how they were made.

Feign then what's by a decent tact believed
And act that state is only so conceived,
  And build an edifice of form
  For house where phantoms may keep warm.

Imagine, then, by miracle, with me,
(Ambiguous gifts, as what gods give must be)
  What could not possibly be there,
  And learn a style from a despair.

p. 1932   WILLIAM EMPSON

The Conflict

  I sang as one
  Who on the tilting deck sings
  To keep their courage up, though the wave hangs
  That shall cut off their sun.

  And as storm-cocks sing,
  Flinging their natural answer in the wind's teeth,
  And care not if it is waste of breath
  Of birth-carol of spring.   ·

  As the ocean-flyer clings
  To height, to the last drop of spirit driving on,
  While yet ahead is land to be won
  And work for wings.

Singing I was at peace,
Above the clouds, outside the ring;
For sorrow finds a swift release in song
And pride its poise.

Yet living here,
As one between two massing powers I live
Whom neutrality cannot save
Nor occupation cheer.

None such shall be left alive:
The innocent wing is soon shot down
And private stars fade in the blood-red dawn
Where two worlds strive.

The red advance of life
Contracts pride, calls out the common blood,
Beats song into a single blade,
Makes a depth-charge of grief.

Move then with new desires,
For where we used to build and love
Is no man's land, and only ghosts can live
Between two fires.

p. 1933   C. DAY LEWIS

Homage to the British Museum

There is a Supreme God in the ethnological section;
A hollow toad shape, faced with a blank shield.
He needs his belly to include the Pantheon,
Which is inserted through a hole behind.
At the navel, at the points formally stressed, at the organs of
    sense,
Lice glue themselves, dolls, local deities,
His smooth wood creeps with all the creeds of the world.

Attending there let us absorb the cultures of nations
And dissolve into our judgement all their codes.
Then, being clogged with a natural hesitation
(People are continually asking one the way out),
Let us stand here and admit that we have no road.
Being everything, let us admit that is to be something,
Or give ourselves the benefit of the doubt;
Let us offer our pinch of dust all to this God,
And grant his reign over the entire building.

c. 1935   WILLIAM EMPSON

Poems XXX

Sir, no man's enemy, forgiving all
But will his negative inversion, be prodigal:
Send to us power and light, a sovereign touch
Curing the intolerable neural itch,
The exhaustion of weaning, the liar's quinsy,
And the distortions of ingrown virginity.
Prohibit sharply the rehearsed response
And gradually correct the coward's stance;
Cover in time with beams those in retreat
That, spotted, they turn though the reverse were great;
Publish each healer that in city lives
Or country houses at the end of drives;
Harrow the house of the dead; look shining at
New styles of architecture, a change of heart.

c. 1930   W. H. AUDEN

In Death the Eyes are Still

In death the eyes are still
And the folds about the eyes
Settle, and the round ears fill
With silence, and the mouth replies
No more, accepting all.

These ghosts who walk, have died
Long since, of life's negation,
Being satisfied
To lapse in their imperfect station
Turning their face to the wall.

We climb the air, to find
An exit from the plaster
Of time: if once the mind's
Propeller slacken, the hollow past
Receives us and we fall.

p. 1934   RANDALL SWINGLER

No Remedy

Smite the devil underground;
It blooms with danger all around.
Or put a stone and write on it
Hic Anti-Christus obiit.
The verb is nothing, but the name
Remains triumphant and the same.
Set a priest against a witch;
They mirror until who knows which?
Boast you have cut out evil; but
What is the outline round the cut?

What hieroglyph remains to teach
You letters of unholy speech?
Smite and declaim and cut away;
There he was, and there he'll stay.

p. 1933   NORMAN CAMERON

May with its Light Behaving

May with its light behaving
Stirs vessel, eye, and limb;
The singular and sad
Are willing to recover,
And to the swan-delighting river
The careless picnics come,
The living white and red.

The dead remote and hooded
In their enclosures rest; but we
From the vague woods have broken,
Forests where children meet
And the white angel-vampires flit;
We stand with shaded eye,
The dangerous apple taken.

The real world lies before us,
Animal motions of the young,
The common wish for death,
The pleasured and the haunted;
The dying master sinks tormented
In the admirers' ring;
The unjust walk the earth.

And love that makes impatient
The tortoise and the roe, and lays
The blonde beside the dark,
Urges upon our blood,
Before the evil and the good
How insufficient is
The endearment and the look.

c. 1936   W. H. AUDEN

The Magnetic Mountain

24

Tempt me no more; for I
Have known the lightning's hour,
The poet's inward Pride,
The certainty of Power.

Bayonets are closing round.
I shrink; yet I must wring
A living from despair
And out of steel a song.

Though song, though breath be short,
I'll share not the disgrace
Of those that ran away
Or never left the base.

Comrades, my tongue can speak
No comfortable words,
Calls to a forlorn hope,
Gives work and not rewards.

Oh keep the sickle sharp
And follow still the plough:
Others may reap, though some
See not the winter through.

Father, who endest all,
Pity our broken sleep:
For we lie down with tears
And waken but to weep.

And if our blood alone
Will melt this iron earth,
Take it. It is well spent
Easing a saviour's birth.

c. 1933   C. DAY LEWIS

An Eclogue for Christmas

A. I meet you in an evil time.

B.   The evil bells
   Put out of our heads, I think, the thought of everything
      else.
A. The jaded calendar revolves,
   Its nuts need oil, carbon chokes the valves,
   The excess sugar of a diabetic culture
   Rotting the nerve of life and literature;
   Therefore when we bring out the old tinsel and frills
   To announce that Christ is born among the barbarous
      hills
   I turn to you whom a morose routine
   Saves from the mad vertigo of being what has been.
B. Analogue of me, you are wrong to turn to me,
   My country will not yield you any sanctuary,
   There is no pinpoint in any of the ordnance maps
   To save you when your towns and town-bred thoughts
      collapse,
   It is better to die in situ as I shall,
   One place is as bad as another. Go back where your in-
      stincts call

205

And listen to the crying of the town-cats and the taxis
   again,
Or wind your gramophone and eavesdrop on great men.
A. Jazz-weary of years of drums and Hawaiian guitar
Pivoting on the parquet I seem to have moved far
From bombs and mud and gas have stuttered on my feet
Clinched to the streamlined and butter-smooth trulls of
   the élite,
The lights irritating and gyrating and rotating in gauze –
Pomade-dazzle, a slick beauty of gewgaws –
I who was Harlequin in the childhood of the century
Posed by Picasso beside an endless opaque sea
Have seen myself sifted and splintered in broken facets
Tentative pencillings, endless liabilities, no assets,
Abstractions scalpelled with a palette-knife
Without reference to this particular life.
And so it has gone on, I have not been allowed to be
Myself in flesh or face, but abstracting and dissecting me
They have made of me pure form, a symbol or a pastiche,
Stylized profile, anything but soul and flesh :
And that is why I turn this jaded music on
To forswear thought and become an automaton.
B. There are in the country also of whom I am afraid –
Men who put beer into a belly that is dead,
Women in the forties with terrier and setter who whistle
   and swank
Over down and plough and Roman road and daisied
   bank
Half-conscious that these barriers over which they stride
Are nothing to the barbed wire that has grown round
   their pride.
A. And two there are, as I drive in the city, who suddenly
   perturb –
The one sirening me to draw up by the kerb
The other, as I lean back, my right leg stretched creating
   speed,

Making me catch and stamp, the brakes shrieking, pull
    up dead:
She wears silk stockings taunting the winter wind,
He carries a white stick to mark that he is blind.

B. In the country they are still hunting, in the heavy shires
Greyness is on the fields and sunset like a line of pyres
Of barbarous heroes smoulders through the ancient air
Hazed with factory dust and, orange opposite, the
    moon's glare,
Goggling yokel-stubborn through the iron trees,
Jeers at the end of us, our bland ancestral ease;
We shall go down like palaeolithic man
Before some new Ice Age or Genghiz Khan.

A. It is time for some new coinage, people have got so old,
Hacked and handled and shiny from pocketing they have
    made bold
To think that each is himself through these accidents,
    being blind
To the fact that they are merely the counters of an un-
    known Mind.

B. A Mind that does not think, if such a thing can be,
Mechanical Reason, capricious Identity.
That I could be able to face this domination nor flinch –

A. The tin toys of the hawker move on the pavement inch
    by inch
Not knowing that they are wound up; it is better to be
    so
Than to be, like us, wound up and while running down
    to know.

B. But everywhere the pretence of individuality recurs –
A. Old faces frosted with powder and choked in furs
B. The jutlipped farmer gazing over the humpbacked wall
A. The commercial traveller joking in the urinal
B. I think things draw to an end, the soil is stale
A. And over-elaboration will nothing now avail,
The street is up again, gas, electricity or drains,

Ever-changing conveniences, nothing comfortable re-
mains
Un-improved, as flagging Rome improved villa and
sewer
(A sound-proof library and a stable temperature)
Our street is up, red lights sullenly mark
The long trench of pipes, iron guts in the dark,
And not till the Goths again come swarming down the
hill
Will cease the clangour of the electric drill.
But yet there is beauty narcotic and deciduous
In this vast organism grown out of us,
On all the traffic-islands stand white globes like moons
The city's haze is clouded amber that purrs and croons,
And tilting by the noble curve bus after tall bus comes
With an osculation of yellow light, with a glory like
chrysanthemums.

B. The country gentry cannot change, they will die in their
shoes
From angry circumstance and moral self-abuse
Dying with a paltry fizzle they will prove their lives to be
An ever-diluted drug, a spiritual tautology.
They cannot live once their idols are turned out
None of them can endure, for how could they, possibly,
without
The flotsam of private property, pekingese and polyan-
thus
The good things which in the end turn to poison and pus,
Without the bandy chairs and the sugar in the silver
tongs
And the inter-ripple and resonance of years of dinner
gongs
Or if they could find no more that cumulative proof
In the rain dripping off the conservatory roof?
What will happen when the only sanction the country-
dweller has –

A. What will happen to us, planked and panelled with jazz?

Who go to the theatre where a black man dances like an eel

Where pink thighs flash like the spokes of a wheel, where we feel

That we know in advance all the jogtrot and the cake-walk jokes

All the bumfun and the gags of the comedians in boaters and toques

All the tricks of the virtuosos who invert the usual –

B. What will happen to us when the State takes down the manor wall

When there is no more private shooting or fishing, when the trees are all cut down

When faces are all dials and cannot smile or frown –

A. What will happen when the sniggering machine-guns in the hands of the young men

Are trained on every flat and club and beauty parlour and Father's den?

What will happen when our civilization like a long pent balloon –

B. What will happen will happen; the whore and the buffoon

Will come off best; no dreamers, they cannot lose their dream

And are at least likely to be reinstated in the new régime.

But one thing is not likely –

A.   Do not gloat over yourself

Do not be your own vulture, high on some mountain shelf

Huddle the pitiless abstractions bald about the neck

Who will descend when you crumple in the plains a wreck.

Over the randy of the theatre and cinema I hear songs

Unlike anything –

B.   The lady of the house poises the silver tongs

And picks a lump of sugar, 'ne plus ultra' she says
'I cannot do otherwise, even to prolong my days' –

A. I cannot do otherwise either, tonight I will book my
   seat –

B. I will walk about the farm-yard which is replete
   As with the smell of dung so with memories –

A. I will gorge myself to satiety with the oddities
   Of every artiste, official or amateur,
   Who has pleased me in my role of hero-worshipper
   Who has pleased me in my role of individual man –

B. Let us lie once more, say 'What we think, we can'
   The old idealist lie –

A.   And for me before I die
   Let me go the round of the garish glare –

B.   And on the bare and high
   Places of England, the Wiltshire Downs and the Long
   Mynd
   Let the balls of my feet bounce on the turf, my face burn
   in the wind
   My eyelashes stinging in the wind, and the sheep like
   grey stones
   Humble my human pretensions –

A.   Let the saxophones and the xylophones
   And the cult of every technical excellence, the miles of
   canvas in the galleries
   And the canvas of the rich man's yacht snapping and
   tacking on the seas
   And the perfection of a grilled steak –

B.   Let all these so ephemeral things
   Be somehow permanent like the swallow's tangent wings:
   Good-bye to you, this day remember is Christmas, this
   morn
   They say, interpret it your own way, Christ is born.

p. 1934   LOUIS MACNEICE

VI. WHEN LOGICS DIE

Offering

I offer you my forests and my street-cries
With hands of double patience under the clock;
The antiseptic arguments and lies
Uttered before the flood, the submerged rock;
The sack of meal pierced by the handsome fencer,
The flowers dying for 'a great adventure'.

I offer you the mysterious parable,
The mount of reason, the hero's glassy hymn,
The disquieting uproar of the obvious
Hate in the taproom, murder in the barn,
The long experienced finger of the Gulf Stream,
The flying sense of glory in a failure's dream.

I offer you the bubble of free-will,
The rarefied agony of forgotten places,
The green cadaver stirring to the moon's pull,
The cheerful butchery of raw amateur faces,
Which like the half-blind nags shipped off for food
Die, doubtless serving some higher good.

I offer you the Egyptian miracle,
The acrobat doing handsprings in the rain,
The touched-up photograph in sepia
Of the future teasing the fibres of the brain;
I offer you the seven-league army boots he wears
Striding down the black funnel of the years.

I offer you a coral growth of cells,
A flash of lightning anchored in a carafe.

The withered arm of the last century
Cannot provoke a demon to anger us.
The strap-hanging skeleton of what has been
Is out of date forever like the crinoline.

I offer you clouds of nuisance, fleurs-de-lis,
The opening lips of summer where pigeons rest,
The exploding office of the vast nebula,
The heraldic device under the left breast,
The taut string and the scribbler's Roman tread
Impinging on the slow shores of the dead.

I offer you the tithes of discontent,
The deck-games played with shadows on a cruise
Beyond the islands marked on the ancient maps
With the broken altars, markets in disuse,
To some 'unspoilt' and blessed hemisphere
Where comfort twists the lucid strands of air.

I would offer you so much more if you would turn
Before the new whisper in a forgiving hour.
Let all the wild ones who have offended burn,
Let love dissemble in a golden shower;
Let not the winds whistle, nor the sea rave,
But the treasure be lapped forever in an unbroken wave.

There is nothing that I would not offer you,
My silken dacoit, my untranslatable,
Whether in the smug mountains counting the stars
Or crossing the gipsy's palm in the Easter fairs,
With so much that is so difficult to say
Before the frigid unpeculating hours
Shall drive this foreign devil to the sea.

p. 1936   KENNETH ALLOTT

Poem

The clock ticks on; the wild-fingered hand
of a dark wet evening strokes the face
and combs the hair out-of-doors,
and traffic and expressions are woof and warp
of a cruelly-clear understanding. The people drag a train of
    ancient monsters,
cumbrous shadows with banners
of factory hours and weekly wage. Sirens of contempt
whistle in the incidental phrase
and the metre of a force prepared to impel a change
gives words the white outline of chairs seen in fainting,
here we have a room of drastic furniture waiting the
    remover's approach
(and he comes solemn as two girders
in a bridge, intent as the dead timber floating under it).

No foaming running cloud of the night
can disengage hysteria locked in the pounding heart
slowly rejoining the serene wide-open eye.

p. 1938   PHILIP O'CONNOR

Worm Interviewed

It said it was the resurrection's worm,
Coiling its long whip in the empty vein;
Again, it said, I am the carnal worm
Sprung sweetly from the tissue of the head;
I, and I only, know the marrows of the brain,
The mysterious issue of the infertile egg.

I caused the mind-storm in the summer,
Throwing my long spear in the blood;
I caused the cracking of the missing rib,

215

My teeth the chisel and my eye the hammer.
Being the maggot in the newly dead
I heard the last pulse come bitterly.

I stole the tendon from the fractured foot
As scaffolding to bolster up my hollow nest;
I stole the nerve that held the eye to socket,
Now dropped aimlessly upon the cheek.
I was the asp about the virgin's breast
That made the milk to run at Christmas time.

I was the first thing and am last;
I made the bone that cowered in the womb,
My nest about it made the firm hard limb.
I am the Maker who does not count the cost
Of the long shelter of the shallow tomb.
I am the Priest who battens on the dead.

p. 1936   RUTHVEN TODD

And Death Shall Have No Dominion

And death shall have no dominion.
Dead men naked they shall be one
With the man in the wind and the west moon;
When their bones are picked clean and the clean bones gone,
They shall have stars at elbow and foot;
Though they go mad they shall be sane,
Though they sink through the sea they shall rise again;
Though lovers be lost love shall not;
And death shall have no dominion.

And death shall have no dominion.
Under the windings of the sea
They lying long shall not die windily;

Twisting on racks when sinews give way,
Strapped to a wheel, yet they shall not break;
Faith in their hands shall snap in two,
And the unicorn evils run them through;
Split all ends up they shan't crack;
And death shall have no dominion.

And death shall have no dominion.
No more may gulls cry at their ears
Or waves break loud on the seashores;
Where blew a flower may a flower no more
Lift its head to the blows of the rain;
Though they be mad and dead as nails,
Heads of the characters hammer through daisies;
Break in the sun till the sun breaks down,
And death shall have no dominion.

c. 1936   DYLAN THOMAS

Risorgimento

Not from a new soil
Unchurned by insistent roots,
Not out of any small miraculous seed
Nor plucking timid sustenance with soft fingers in the earth
To be a hieroglyph of growth shown
On fostering air

But like the blessed pilgrim staff
That was dead
And that became alive with many flowers,
Grace in its own hard fibres groping

For emergence is
A deposition of small virginities,
And that obscene virginity
Which squatted on our shoulders like
An old man of the sea with writhing legs
Is clutched and flung down
by hands unhusked.

p. 1933   RAYNER HEPPENSTALL

Figure in a Landscape

The verdant valleys full of rivers
Sang a fresh song to the thirsty hills.
The rivers sang:
'Our mother is the Night, into the Day we flow. The mills
Which toil our waters have no thirst. We flow
Like light.'
                    And the great birds
Which dwell among the rocks, flew down
Into the dales to drink, and their dark wings
Threw flying shades across the pastures green.

At dawn the rivers flowed into the sea.
The mountain birds
Rose out of sleep like a winged cloud, a single fleet,
And flew into a newly-risen sun.

– Anger of the sun: the deadly blood-red rays which strike
    oblique
Through olive branches on the slopes and kill the kine.
– Tears of the sun: the summer evening rains which hang
    grey veils
Between the earth and sky, and soak the corn, and brim the
    lakes.

– Dream of the sun: the mists which swim down from the
   icy heights
And hide the gods who wander on the mountain-sides at
   noon.

The sun was anguished, and the sea
Threw up its crested arms and cried aloud out of the depths;
And the white horses of the waves raced the black horses of
   the clouds;
The rocky peaks clawed at the sky like gnarled imploring
   hands:
And the black cypresses strained upwards like the sex of a
   hanged man.

*

Across the agonizing land there fled
Among the landscape's limbs (the limbs
Of a vast denuded body torn and vanquished from within)
The chaste white road,
Prolonged into the distance like a plaint.

Between the opposition of the night and day
Between the opposition of the earth and sky
Between the opposition of the sea and land
Between the opposition of the landscape and the road
A traveller came
                        Whose only nudity his armour was
Against the whirlwind and the weapon, the undoing wound

And met himself half-way.

Spectre as white as salt in the crude light of the sky
Spectre confronted by flesh, the present and past
Meet timelessly upon the endless road,
Merge timelessly in time and pass away,
Dreamed face away from stricken face into the bourn
Of the unborn, and the real face of age into the fastnesses of
   death.

Infinitely small among the infinitely huge
Drunk with the rising fluids of his breast, his boiling heart,
Exposed and naked as the skeleton – upon his knees
Like some tormented desert saint – he flung
The last curse of regret against Omnipotence.
And the lightning struck his face.

*

After the blow, the bruised earth blooms again,
The storm-wrack, wrack of the cloudy sea
Dissolve, the rocks relax,
As the pallid phallus sinks in the clear dawn
Of a new day, and the wild eyes melt and close,
And the eye of the sun is no more blind –

Clear milk of love, O lave the devastated vale,
And peace of high-noon, soothe the traveller's pain
Whose hands still grope and clutch, whose head
Thrown back entreats the guerison
And music of your light!

The valley rivers irrigate the land, the mills
Revolve, the hills are fecund with the cypress and the vine,
And the great eagles guard the mountain heights.

Above the peaks in mystery there sit
The Presences, the Unseen in the sky,
Inscrutable, whose influences like rays
Descend upon him, pass through and again
Like golden bees the hive of his lost head.

c. 1938   DAVID GASCOYNE

Light Breaks Where No Sun Shines

Light breaks where no sun shines;
Where no sea runs, the waters of the heart
Push in their tides;
And, broken ghosts with glowworms in their heads.
The things of light
File through the flesh where no flesh decks the bones.

A candle in the thighs
Warms youth and seed and burns the seeds of age;
Where no seed stirs,
The fruit of man unwrinkles in the stars,
Bright as a fig;
Where no wax is, the candle shows its hairs.

Dawn breaks behind the eyes;
From poles of skull and toe the windy blood
Slides like a sea;
Nor fenced, nor staked, the gushers of the sky
Spout to the rod
Divining in a smile the oil of tears.

Night in the sockets rounds,
Like some pitch moon, the limit of the globes;
Day lights the bone;
Where no cold is, the skinning gales unpin
The winter's robes;
The film of spring is hanging from the lids.

Light breaks on secret lots,
On tips of thought where thoughts smell in the rain;
When logics die,

The secret of the soil grows through the eye,
And blood jumps in the sun;
Above the waste allotments the dawn halts.

c. 1934   DYLAN THOMAS

Morning Dissertation

Wakening, peering through eye-windows, uncurious, not
    amazed,
Balance the day, know you lie there, think: 'I'm on earth.'
Remember death walks in the daylight and life still through
    filter seeps,
While you will remain unchanged, perhaps, throughout the
    day.
Time like an urgent finger moves across the chart,
But you are you, Time is not yours alone,
You are but one dot on the complex diagram.

Then are you a star, a nucleus, centre of moving points?
Are you a rock-crumb, broken from cliff, alone?
Or are you a point of a greater star, moving in unison?
If you are isolate, only a self, then petrify there where you
    stand;
Destinies crumble, bodies run down, the single sconces burn
    out,
But you are complete if without you completion is lacking,
Then you blaze with the perfect light and are Time's body-
    man.

p. 1933   DAVID GASCOYNE

Three Evils

When the sky has the ominous
Colours of a bruise, even then
Bother less over the spirits from the sky
Than the spirits from the earth:

They are up under your feet
Before the sun goes, they frequent
The urinals, the henbane heap,
The oil patches of the lorry yard.

Be very careful about them,
Be careful about the invalid,
Stubbly, in slack flannel, who
Reclines on the river balcony.

And I warn you last – she is the
Worst evil – against the Sybil,
The rare Marocaine who foresees
Events in a mirror of tar.

p. 1936   GEOFFREY GRIGSON

'Blue Bugs in Liquid Silk'

blue bugs in liquid silk
talk with correlation particularly like
two women in white bandages

a birdcage swings from the spleen of ceiling frowning her
   soul in large wastes
and a purple sound purrs in basket-house
putting rubies on with red arms

enter the coalman in a storm of sacks
holding a queenly egg-cup
the window stares and thinks separately her hair
impartially embankment
to the flood of her thought in motionless torrent
roundly looking the ladies

there is no formula for disruption of pink plaster
nor emotions to bandage the dead

p. 1937   PHILIP O'CONNOR

Before a Fall

And what was the big room he walked in?

> The big room he walked in,
> Over the smooth floor,
> Under the sky light,
> Was his own brain.

And what was it he admired there?

> He admired there
> The oval mirror.

And what was it the oval mirror showed him there?

> It showed him the roots
> Through the ceiling,
> The gross armchair, the bookcase
> Shuttered with glass,
> The Hymns bound in velvet,
> The porcelain oven,
> The giant egg cups,
> The hairy needles,
> And the silence –

And the smell of smouldering dung
Hung between the walls
(Which were yellow as dandelion).

And how did he leave?

On the smooth floor
His neat feet jarred
And his teeth grew down
To his heart, and he slipped
On the white stairhead –

Which ended?

Which ended in coldness
And darkness,
Through which he fell
(So they tell)
With little hope, and slowly.

p. 1936   GEOFFREY GRIGSON

Twenty-four Years Remind the Tears of My Eyes

Twenty-four years remind the tears of my eyes.
(Bury the dead for fear that they walk to the grave in
    labour.)
In the groin of the natural doorway I crouched like a tailor
Sewing a shroud for a journey
By the light of the meat-eating sun.
Dressed to die, the sensual strut begun,
With my red veins full of money,
In the final direction of the elementary town
I advance for as long as forever is.

c. 1939   DYLAN THOMAS

I

From *Petron*

III, 2, (vi)

In the midst of a ravaged city, the returned exile stands by the ruins of his ancient home. The blood of his slaughtered father has long been washed away by the rains, all traces of habitation have long been obliterated, and nothing remains but a heap of shattered stones where the lizards dart and snakes find shelter.

Searching among the rubble, he finds a battered toy that was once his own, but even as he holds it, it stirs in his hand and becomes a grasshopper, then an old man, a monstrous spider, a woman's breast, a bunch of faded grass, a little heap of bones, and so to a lizard which eludes his grasp, and darts away among the sunlit stones.

c. 1935   HUGH SYKES DAVIES

From *Petron*

III, 2, (i)

A spider weaves his web upon a gibbet.
A second spider weaves his web upon the same gibbet.
And a third.
With three more, all spiders, weaving their webs upon the same gibbet.
Then the seventh spider would seem to be the one at large. No! see, there he weaves, there he weaves, the shadow of a web upon the shadow,
the shadow of the same gibbet.

c. 1935   HUGH SYKES DAVIES

Poem

In the stump of the old tree, where the heart has rotted out,/there is a hole the length of a man's arm, and a dank pool at the/bottom of it where the rain gathers, and the old leaves turn into/lacy skeletons. But do not put your hand down to see, because

in the stumps of old trees, where the hearts have rotted out,/there are holes the length of a man's arm, and dank pools at the/bottom where the rain gathers and old leaves turn to lace, and the/beak of a dead bird gapes like a trap. But do not put your/hand down to see, because

in the stumps of old trees with rotten hearts, where the rain/gathers and the laced leaves and the dead bird like a trap, there/are holes the length of a man's arm, and in every crevice of the/rotten wood grow weasel's eyes like molluscs, their lids open/and shut with the tide. But do not put your hand down to see, because

in the stumps of old trees where the rain gathers and the/ trapped leaves and the beak, and the laced weasel's eyes, there are/holes the length of a man's arm, and at the bottom a sodden bible/written in the language of rooks. But do not put your hand down/to see, because

in the stumps of old trees where the hearts have rotted out there are holes the length of a man's arm where the weasels are/trapped and the letters of the rook language are laced on the/sodden leaves, and at the bottom there is a man's arm. But do/not put your hand down to see, because

in the stumps of old trees where the hearts have rotted out/
there are deep holes and dank pools where the rain gathers,
and/if you ever put your hand down to see, you can wipe it
in the/sharp grass till it bleeds, but you'll never want to eat
with/it again.

p. 1936   HUGH SYKES DAVIES

The Force that Through the Green Fuse

The force that through the green fuse drives the flower
Drives my green age; that blasts the roots of trees
Is my destroyer.
And I am dumb to tell the crooked rose
My youth is bent by the same wintry fever.

The force that drives the water through the rocks
Drives my red blood; that dries the mouthing streams
Turns mine to wax.
And I am dumb to mouth unto my veins
How at the mountain spring the same mouth sucks.

The hand that whirls the water in the pool
Stirs the quicksand; that ropes the blowing wind
Hauls my shroud sail.
And I am dumb to tell the hanging man
How of my clay is made the hangman's lime.

The lips of time leech to the fountain head;
Love drips and gathers, but the fallen blood
Shall calm her sores.
And I am dumb to tell a weather's wind
How time has ticked a heaven round the stars.

And I am dumb to tell the lover's tomb
How at my sheet goes the same crooked worm.

c. 1934   DYLAN THOMAS

And the Seventh Dream is the Dream of Isis

I

white curtains of infinite fatigue
dominating the starborn heritage of the colonies of St
    Francis
white curtains of tortured destinies
inheriting the calamities of the plagues of the desert
encourage the waistlines of women to expand
and the eyes of men to enlarge like pocket-cameras
teach children to sin at the age of five
to cut out the eyes of their sisters with nail-scissors
to run into the streets and offer themselves to unfrocked
    priests
teach insects to invade the deathbeds of rich spinsters
and to engrave the foreheads of their footmen with purple
    signs
for the year is open the year is complete
the year is full of unforeseen happenings
and the time of earthquakes is at hand

today is the day when the streets are full of hearses
and when women cover their ring fingers with pieces of silk
when the doors fall off their hinges in ruined cathedrals
when hosts of white birds fly across the ocean from america
and make their nests in the trees of public gardens
the pavements of cities are covered with needles
the reservoirs are full of human hair
fumes of sulphur envelop the houses of ill-fame
out of which bloodred lilies appear.

across the square where crowds are dying in thousands
a man is walking a tightrope covered with moths

2

there is an explosion of geraniums in the ballroom of the
    hotel
there is an extremely unpleasant odour of decaying meat
arising from the depetalled flower growing out of her ear
her arms are like pieces of sandpaper
or wings of leprous birds in taxis
and when she sings her hair stands on end
and lights itself with a million little lamps like glowworms
you must always write the last two letters of her christian
    name
upside down with a blue pencil

she was standing at the window clothed only in a ribbon
she was burning the eyes of snails in a candle
she was eating the excrement of dogs and horses
she was writing a letter to the president of france

the edges of leaves must be examined through microscopes
in order to see the stains made by dying flies
at the other end of the tube is a woman bathing her husband
and a box of newspapers covered with handwriting
when an angel writes the word TOBACCO across the sky
the sea becomes covered with patches of dandruff
the trunks of trees burst open to release streams of milk
little girls stick photographs of genitals to the windows of
    their homes
prayerbooks in churches open themselves at the death service
and virgins cover their parents' bed with tealeaves
there is an extraordinary epidemic of tuberculosis in york-
    shire
where medical dictionaries are banned from the public
    libraries
and salt turns a pale violet colour every day at seven o'clock
when the hearts of troubadours unfold like soaked mat-
    tresses
when the leaven of the gruesome slum-visitors
and the wings of private airplanes look like shoeleather
shoeleather on which pentagrams have been drawn
shoeleather covered with vomitings of hedgehogs
shoeleather used for decorating wedding-cakes
and the gums of queens like glass marbles
queens whose wrists are chained to the walls of houses
and whose fingernails are covered with little drawings of
    flowers
we rejoice to receive the blessing of criminals
and we illuminate the roofs of convents when they are hung
we look through a telescope on which the lord's prayer has
    been written
and we see an old woman making a scarecrow
on a mountain near a village in the middle of spain
we see an elephant killing a stag-beetle

by letting hot tears fall onto the small of its back
we see a large cocoa-tin full of shapeless lumps of wax
there is a horrible dentist walking out of a ship's funnel
and leaving behind him footsteps which make noises
on account of his accent he was discharged from the sana-
    torium
and sent to examine the methods of cannibals
so that wreaths of passion-flowers were floating in the dark-
    ness
giving terrible illnesses to the possessors of pistols
so that large quantities of rats disguised as pigeons
were sold to various customers from neighbouring towns
who were adepts at painting gothic letters on screens
and at tying up parcels with pieces of grass
we told them to cut off the buttons on their trousers
but they swore in our faces and took off their shoes
whereupon the whole place was stifled with vast clouds of
    smoke
and with theatres and eggshells and droppings of eagles
and the drums of the hospitals were broken like glass
and glass were the faces in the last looking-glass.

p. 1933   DAVID GASCOYNE

Useful Letter

You mustn't take in more idealism than you can usefully
    digest. It's like these –
these fingers, that gallant
compact head and the flowing hair that's just frittered away
    on useless trifles like the wind or an allowance of sunset.
Everything has its place, like the charwoman in her box of
    essential clothes and qualifications or the gentleman
    poured down *his* sartorial chimney.

And that necromancer – the baby with chuckling digits
gurgling round a new, splendid, *shining* gadget released
from the dark storm.

Allow their minds,

my brother in prison

with the hair-steel bars,

launched into this pitiful world. Allow their self-absorbing
drama of foibles. The stuffed lion, Personality. How
deliciously it trickles on the slopes of chaos – how pretty!
Rain, gentle, wayward on the ruins. I see the Character
dribbling his charming self on a shuddering city. I see
him ensconced on a throne of the past right in the midst
of, no doubt honouring *us* rubbish heaps.

Long live these resilient blades, my demon.

There is room for everything. The Pied Piper of Hamelin
disturbed all this – with a magic tune.

Linger in your chair, you

swinging above leprous beauty (chunks of these bodies
chaunting, performing, flaunting in anarchy, with each
sweaty and tired edge bidding his partner a nose-
thumbing good-bye. I'm sure a ruin enjoys itself as much
as the human plastered assemblages.)

A gentleman is a fine thing. I think,

you know,

he has parts. Yes, I have an *intuition*

(and this only when I am in a dark room with my private
African Congo tribe rioting around)

to this effect. Neither, on a sultry day, would I be *convinced*
of this most interesting, yet slightly academic

AMONGST OURSELVES

YOU UNDERSTAND! – fact. He is mobile. He announces,
denounces, considers. He is struck with an idea, and

about this

my old tomcat (Cecil Rhodes)

tells me he does something. O with certain injury to his
health but how *heroic* is a gentleman to put up with this
and re-experience the injury.

All in all, my fiend to whom I send this letter,
I think there is room for everything and that everything has
a place.
BUT
You must not take on (be impregnated with)
more ideals than you can profitably digest. Nosir.

p. 1938   PHILIP O'CONNOR

The Very Image

to René Magritte

An image of my grandmother
her head appearing upside-down upon a cloud
the cloud transfixed on the steeple
of a deserted railway-station
far away

An image of an aqueduct
with a dead crow hanging from the first arch
a modern-style chair from the second
a fir-tree lodged in the third
and the whole scene sprinkled with snow

An image of the piano-tuner
with a basket of prawns on his shoulder
and a firescreen under his arm
his moustache made of clay-clotted twigs
and his cheeks daubed with wine

An image of an aeroplane
the propeller is rashers of bacon
the wings are of reinforced lard
the tail is made of paper-clips
the pilot is a wasp

An image of the painter
with his left hand in a bucket
and his right hand stroking a cat
as he lies in bed
with a stone beneath his head

And all these images
and many others
are arranged like waxworks
in model bird-cages
about six inches high.

p. 1936   DAVID GASCOYNE

Soluble Noughts and Crosses

OR

California, Here I Come

In a small theodolite of paper
I could see the eyelash of a girl,
The most beautiful young girl of all,
Who was only dressed in cellophane,
Who was speaking from a stone
And saying this to me:
'Look out for the red and written triangle,
And enclose a penny-halfpenny stamp;
For I must go at ten to one,
Ten to one it's guineas time,

Ten to one will be too many,
Ten to one you'll come in last.
Yes, did you hear:
My fingers hang like pictures,
And my breasts are pointing to the North?'

So I made an expedition to the Pole,
While thin birds flew off sideways with a sob;
There I heard a ringing at the door,
Where some gongs were waiting in a queue;
I played them all in turn
And presently she stepped out from a handbag,
Saying this to me:
'The happy compass is decided,
I must come at ten to one,
Ten to one's beginner's time,
Ten to one won't be enough,
Ten to one we'll get there first.
Please take this down,
Yes take this down, for purple trees will sing the answer,
For rhyming trains are meeting at a foxtrot,
For string is floating on the water,
For we are opening a parcel meant for both;
Yes please take this down, for living words are played
    together,
For love has grown up like a hair.'

p. 1936   ROGER ROUGHTON

I see the Boys of Summer

I

I see the boys of summer in their ruin
Lay the gold tithings barren,
Setting no store by harvest freeze the soils;
There in their heat the winter floods
Of frozen loves they fetch their girls,
And drown the cargoed apples in their tides.

These boys of light are curdlers in their folly,
Sour the boiling honey;
The jacks of frost they finger in the hives;
There in the sun the frigid threads
Of doubt and dark they feed their nerves;
The signal moon is zero in their voids.

I see the summer children in their mothers
Split up the brawned womb's weathers,
Divide the night and day with fairy thumbs;
There in the deep with quartered shades
Of sun and moon they paint their dams
As sunlight paints the shelling of their heads.

I see that from these boys shall men of nothing
Stature by seedy shifting
Or lame the air with leaping from its heats;
There from their hearts the dogdayed pulse
Of love and light bursts in their throats.
Oh see the pulse of summer in the ice.

But seasons must be challenged or they totter
Into a chiming quarter
Where, punctual as death, we ring the stars;
There, in his night, the black-tongued bells
The sleepy man of winter pulls,
Nor blows back moon-and-midnight as she blows.

We are the dark deniers, let us summon
Death from a summer woman,
A muscling life from lovers in their cramp,
From the fair dead who flush the sea
The bright-eyed worm on Davy's lamp,
And from the planted womb the man of straw.

We summer boys in this four-winded spinning,
Green of the seaweeds' iron,
Hold up the noisy sea and drop her birds,
Pick the world's ball of wave and froth
To choke the deserts with her tides,
And comb the county gardens for a wreath.

In spring we cross our foreheads with the holly,
Heigh-ho the blood and berry,
And nail the merry squires to the trees;
Here love's damp muscle dries and dies,
Here break a kiss in no love's quarry.
Oh see the poles of promise in the boys.

3
I see you boys of summer in your ruin.
Man in his maggot's barren.
And boys are full and foreign in the pouch.
I am the man your father was.
We are the sons of flint and pitch.
Oh see the poles are kissing as they cross.

p. 1934   DYLAN THOMAS

Animal Crackers in Your Croup

I have told you that there is a laugh in every corner
And a pocket-book stuffed with rolls of skin
To pay off the bills of the costive
To buy a new pipe for the dog
To send a committee to bury a stone

I have told you all this
But do you know that
Tomorrow the palmist will lunch on his crystal
Tomorrow REVOLT will be written in human hair
Tomorrow the hangman's rope will tie itself in a bow
Tomorrow virginia creeper will strangle the clergy
Tomorrow the witness will tickle the judge
Tomorrow this page will be found in a womb
Tomorrow the lovers will answer the palace
Tomorrow Karl Marx will descend in a fire-balloon
Tomorrow the word that you lost will ask you home
Tomorrow the virgin will fall down a magnified well
Tomorrow the news will be broadcast in dialect
Tomorrow the beautiful girl will attend
Tomorrow a cloud will follow the bankers
Tomorrow a child will rechristen our London as LONDON
Tomorrow a tree will grow into a hand
Yes listen
Tomorrow the clocks will chime like voices
Tomorrow a train will set out for the sky

National papers please reprint
p. 1936   ROGER ROUGHTON

Lady Windermere's Fan-Dance

Figures and trees in the street
Are stretching and waving their arms,
Reaching the time to repeat
The errors: result of alarms

Earlier heard in the night,
Reports they once read on a wall.
Fingers still feeling the light
Remember the hours of the fall

When gently no one had saved
With fingers in fingers of one,
Hands from the barricades waved
Or hands in the dark when they won.

Sulphurous clouds from the bank
Are killing the quick in the stream,
Bodies from gunboats that sank
Are menacing guns with a dream;

Wavering over the sun
Their arms are still greeting a king,
Holding out hands for a gun,
Impatient for shadows to spring.

Arms of the fighters of tin
And hands of the brave of a thought
Signal the time to begin
By quietly dividing by nought.

p. 1936   ROGER ROUGHTON

Should Lanterns Shine

Should lanterns shine, the holy face,
Caught in an octagon of unaccustomed light,
Would wither up, and any boy of love
Look twice before he fell from grace,
The features in their private dark
Are formed of flesh, but let the false day come
And from her lips the faded pigments fall,
The mummy cloths expose an ancient breast.

I have been told to reason by the heart,
But heart, like head, leads helplessly;
I have been told to reason by the pulse,
And, when it quickens, alter the actions' pace
Till field and roof lie level and the same,
So fast I move defying time, the quiet gentleman
Whose beard wags in Egyptian wind.

I have heard many years of telling,
And many years should see some change.

The ball I threw while playing in the park
Has not yet reached the ground.

Regard the moon, it hangs above the lawn;
Regard the lawn, it lies beneath the moon.

p. 1935   DYLAN THOMAS

Poems

5

Captain Busby put his beard in his mouth and sucked it,
    then took it out and spat on it then put it in and
    sucked it then walked on down the street thinking
    hard.
Suddenly he put his wedding ring in his trilby hat and put
    the hat on a passing kitten. Then he carefully cal-
    culated the width of the pavement with a pair of
    adjustable sugar-tongs. This done he knitted his
    brows. Then he walked on thinking hard.

6

Captain Busted Busby frowned hard at a passing ceiling and
    fixed his eye upon a pair of stationary taxis. Suddenly
    he went up to one of them and addressed himself to
    the driver. He discharged his socks and continued
    whistling. The taxi saluted but he put up with it, and
    puckered a resigned mouth and knitted a pair of
    thoughtful eyebrows.

7

M. looking out of his window with purple curtains saw Cap-
    tain Busby thoughtfully chewing a less impatient
    portion of his walking-stick ostentatiously against a
    lamp-post. The road was blue but Captain Busby
    seemed a very dark green with ivory face (for it was
    night time). He frowned. He looked up to the top
    of the rapidly emptying street. He cut his hair slowly.
    He looked at the bottom of the street. He made rapid
    measurements with a pair of adjustable sugar-tongs.
    These he afterwards secreted in his trousers. He then
    flew into his friend's apartment through the willingly
    opened window.

8

Marcella waited for her lover outside a public house known
to both of them. Immediately Captain Busby ap-
peared holding a woman in his arms. This wasn't
true thought Marcella carefully, and was relieved to
see that God had thrown a lamp-post at the Captain,
temporarily disabling him.

9

He arranged himself in sugar and put himself in his bath
And prepared to breathe his last

his four bottles lay grouped around him

do your duty in this world and gather dividends from the
dog thrown at you

goodbye my children

and he died and they huskily nailed down his coffin
and put it in ten feet of soil
and grouped around him reading the will

for indeed and forever would he be
to them
just dad

10

Mother lay crying in the withdrawing room
bitterly bewailing cruel fate who with a flick of his pen
had so completely shattered the even tenour of her ways

sobbed upon the brick platform shaking her fist at every
        porter who passed
declaring cruel fate who with a flick of his pen
had so cruelly broken
the even tenour of her ways

she considered the porter with the cap on the side of his
    head fitfully
who had squandered his sweet-peas upon her
who had ridden every train and blown all whistles
to feast his evil frontal eyes on her to break the even tenour
    of her ways
she shunted her back to him
she put on her large black hat with insolent vulgarity
and deliberately smirked into his face

he was busy
he was doing his duty
he rattled the cans
he gave out composed answers to the backchat following his
    curt commands
he went on with his duty forgetting
that he had broken the even tenour of her ways

She walked thoughtfully upon a sugar-box
and would there and then have harangued the station
    officials to compel the attention of the porter

but he did not
but he could not
but he did not
and could not should as he had broken the even tenour of
    her ways
she thrust a carrot into his face
he gravely took it and handed it without moving a muscle
    of his face
to the dominant personality of
the station master himself

events moved indefatigably to their long-awaited climax
the station master seized the carrot and conveyed it to a
    drawer
reserved for matters of importance
and seizing a document asserting his credentials and authority
motored along the platform and alighted at the lady

madam he said coldly
your carrot is in the drawer
pray come for it or suitable measures will be taken to enforce
the union of yourself and the personality
who broke the even tenour of your ways

lightning juggled above the station portraying its grim
    battlements
thunder crashed upon the assembled people
she threw three flashes of self possessed rays
at him from her large radiant eyes
she ran to the drawer refusing the automobile
she snatched abruptly at the carrot
scenting with inexorable female intuition the precise posi-
    tions afforded by reason of its pre-eminent signifi-
    cance
she ran from the room like a bitten wounded thing
and fell laughing upon the station master who had broken
the even
tenour of her ways

p. 1937   PHILIP O'CONNOR

VII. HAIR BETWEEN THE TOES

The Witnesses

I

You dowagers with Roman noses
Sailing along between banks of roses
   well dressed,
You Lords who sit at committee tables
And crack with grooms in riding stables
   your father's jest;

Solicitors with poker faces,
And doctors with black bags to cases
   hurried,
Reporters coming home at dawn
And heavy bishops on the lawn
   by sermons worried;

You stokers lit by furnace-glare,
And you, too, steeplejacks up there
   singing,
You shepherds wind-blown on the ridges,
Tramps leaning over village bridges
   your eardrums ringing;

On land, on sea, in field, in town
Attend: Musician put them down,
   those trumpets;
Let go, young lover, of her hand
Come forward both of you and stand
   as still as limpets

Close as you can and listen well
My companion here is about to tell
      a story;
Peter, Pontius Pilate, Paul
Whoever you are, it concerns you all
        and human glory.

II

Call him Prince Alpha if you wish
He was born in a palace, his people were swish;
        his christening
Was called by the *Tatler* the event of the year,
All the photographed living were there
        and the dead were listening.

You would think I was trying to foozle you
If I told you all that kid could do;
        enough
To say he was never afraid of the dark
He climbed all the trees in his pater's park;
        his nurse thought him rough.

At school his brilliance was a mystery,
All languages, science, maths, and history
        he knew;
His style at cricket was simply stunning
At rugger, soccer, hockey, running
        and swimming too

The days went by, he grew mature;
He was a looker you may be sure,
        so straight
Old couples cried 'God bless my soul
I thought that man was a telegraph pole'
        when he passed their gate.

His eyes were blue as a mountain lake,
He made the hearts of the girls to ache;
      he was strong;
He was gay, he was witty, his speaking voice
Sounded as if a large Rolls-Royce
      had passed along.

He kissed his dear old mater one day,
He said to her 'I'm going away,
      good-bye'
No sword nor terrier by his side
He set off through the world so wide
      under the sky.

Where did he travel? Where didn't he travel
Over the ice and over the gravel
      and the sea;
Up the fevered jungle river,
Through haunted forests without a shiver
      he wandered free.

What did he do? What didn't he do,
He rescued maidens, overthrew
      ten giants
Like factory chimneys, slaughtered dragons,
Though their heads were larger than railway waggons
      tamed their defiance.

What happened, what happened? I'm coming to that;
He came to a desert and down he sat
      and cried,
Above the blue sky arching wide
Two tall rocks as black as pride
      on either side.

There on a stone he sat him down,
Around the desert stretching brown
      like the tide,
Above the blue sky arching wide
Two black rocks on either side
      and, O how he cried.

'I thought my strength could know no stemming
But I was foolish as a lemming;
      for what
Was I born, was it only to see
I'm as tired of life as life of me?
      let me be forgot.

Children have heard of my every action
It gives me no sort of satisfaction
      and why?
Let me get this as clear as I possibly can
No, I am not the truly strong man,
      O let me die.'

There in the desert all alone
He sat for hours on a long flat stone
      and sighed;
Above the blue sky arching wide
Two black rocks on either side,
      and then he died.

Now ladies and gentlemen, big and small,
This story of course has a morale;
      again
Unless like him you wish to die
Listen, while my friend and I
      proceed to explain.

III

What had he done to be treated thus?
If you want to know, he'd offended us:
      for yes,
We guard the wells, we're handy with a gun,
We've a very special sense of fun,
      we curse and bless.

You are the town, and we are the clock,
We are the guardians of the gate in the rock,
      the Two;
On your left, and on your right
In the day, and in the night
      we are watching you.

Wiser not to ask just what has occurred
To them that disobeyed our word;
      to those
We were the whirlpool, we were the reef,
We were the formal nightmare, grief,
      and the unlucky rose.

Climb up the cranes, learn the sailors' words
When the ships from the islands, laden with birds
      come in;
Tell your stories of fishing and other men's wives,
The expansive moments of constricted lives,
      in the lighted inn.

By all means say of the peasant youth
'That person there is in the truth'
      we're kind
Tire of your little rut and look it,
You have to obey but you don't have to like it,
      we do not mind:

But do not imagine we do not know
Or that what you hide with care won't show
        at a glance;
Nothing is done, nothing is said
But don't make the mistake of thinking us dead;
        I shouldn't dance

For I'm afraid in that case you'll have a fall;
We've been watching you over the garden wall
        for hours,
The sky is darkening like a stain,
Something is going to fall like rain
        and it won't be flowers.

When the green field comes off like a lid
Revealing what were much better hid,
        unpleasant;
And look! behind without a sound
The woods have come up and are standing round
        in deadly crescent.

And the bolt is sliding in its groove,
Outside the window is the black remover's
        van,
And now with sudden swift emergence
Come the women in dark glasses, the hump-backed
  surgeons
        and the scissor-man.

This might happen any day
So be careful what you say
        or do
Be clean, be tidy, oil the lock,
Trim the garden, wind the clock
        Remember the Two.

p. 1933   W. H. AUDEN

End of a City

Birds in the pattern of a constellation,
Blank pale blue sky, white walls of a citadel,
Silence of country without inhabitants.
The shining aqueducts, elaborate drains,
Puffed fountains cleanse a sheeted culture
Where the greatest movement is the soft
Wear of stone by water that leaves no trace
Of green, coming from static glaciers.

By night in the city, stars like heraldic birds,
The square, the plinth with the sacred articles,
The statue of the shade of Spartacus,
No change appears, the cooling is unheard
Of monuments of easy living in
The dark air. But the crack is widening
Between the sun and moon, the rest and flow,
The vomatorium and immense sewers.

Somewhere between and out of time, a flare
Will suddenly cast the shadow of a nose,
Gone with disease, across the praying mouth.
Those aquiline thrown lights will follow, gods
Dissolve like snowmen and the stiff pavement jerk
Its sharp plane upwards. Fragments of the thing
Brought down at first will after choke the outlets,
Force horror through the floor of private places.

See how the separate layers come to life.
The sloping theatre rolls down its bodies
To mingle with the last act's tragedy
Upon the stage, from tarnished bed both king
And mistress tumble, pens fall from the hands

Of nerveless bureaucrats and, rubbing sockets
Of eyeless skulls, the naked slaves awake,
Who face another epoch of draining work.

Within the temple sits the noble JA,
Bearded with seaweed and his elephant's legs
Crossed in the droppings. The lamp has long gone out,
The offerings are mouldy and the priests
Dust in the chancel. This was he who ordered
For his tremendous dropsy the sanitation,
But whose emissaries sent timely hence
Brought no green leaf to soothe his helplessness.

This day is surely lucky for the city.
The last trumpet blown with leaking cheeks
Rouses the oldest tenants from their sleep.
They are the ancestors whose tombs were levelled
At the last cataclysm, but they come
Like grass between the stones, but grass like hair
And growing goatishly along the sewers,
Over the stage, the temple and on JA.

c. 1939   ROY FULLER

Christina

It all began so easy
With bricks upon the floor
Building motley houses
And knocking down your houses
And always building more.

The doll was called Christina,
Her under-wear was lace,
She smiled while you dressed her
And when you then undressed her
She kept a smiling face.

Until the day she tumbled
And broke herself in two
And her legs and arms were hollow
And her yellow head was hollow
Behind her eyes of blue.

. . . .

He went to bed with a lady
Somewhere seen before
He heard the name Christina
And suddenly saw Christina
Dead on the nursery floor.

July, 1939   LOUIS MACNEICE

The Compassionate Fool

My enemy had bidden me as guest.
His table all set out with wine and cake,
His ordered chairs, he to beguile me dressed
So neatly, moved my pity for his sake.

I knew it was an ambush, but could not
Leave him to eat his cake up by himself
And put his unused glasses on the shelf.
I made pretence of falling in his plot,

And trembled when in his anxiety
He bared it too absurdly to my view;
And even as he stabbed me through and through
I pitied him for his small strategy.

p. 1934   NORMAN CAMERON

The Inheritor

Who would have thought the old man had so much blood
So many guts, such yards and yards of guts?
Out of the bucket they trailed in raw festoons
The hungry dog licked at the clammy tubes
And Arnold worked at his un-neat dissection.

Who would have thought one old man went so far?
The sink still gurgled with eternal blood
The bread-bin overflowed its choppered bones
Elusive gristle slithered on the floor
And Arnold dealt with the part that fathered him.

Who would have thought this job would take so long?
For days the copper boiled, the furnace raged
While father billowed forth in obscene smoke
The dog grew sleek with unaccustomed meat
And Arnold at night went on mysterious journeys.

Who would have thought a corpse would cling so hard?
Fragments of father under the finger-nails
Particles in the hair, in the trouser turn-up
But even the skull at last was disposed of secretly
And Arnold lay in the bath content and singing.

Who would have thought this thing would be so simple?
The suit of clothes found on the sea-shore
The empty inquest returning the wished-for verdict
The lawyer discreetly cracking his finger joints
And Arnold in black claiming his heritage.

p. 1938   GEOFFREY PARSONS

Ballad

O what is that sound which so thrills the ear
  Down in the valley drumming, drumming?
Only the scarlet soldiers, dear,
    The soldiers coming.

O what is that light I see flashing so clear
  Over the distance brightly, brightly?
Only the sun on their weapons, dear,
    As they step lightly.

O what are they doing with all that gear;
  What are they doing this morning, this morning?
Only the usual manœuvres, dear,
    Or perhaps a warning.

O why have they left the road down there;
  Why are they suddenly wheeling, wheeling?
Perhaps a change in the orders, dear;
    Why are you kneeling?

O haven't they stopped for the doctor's care;
  Haven't they reined their horses, their horses?
Why, they are none of them wounded, dear,
    None of these forces.

O is it the parson they want, with white hair;
  Is it the parson, is it, is it?
No, they are passing his gateway, dear,
    Without a visit.

O it must be the farmer who lives so near,
  It must be the farmer, so cunning, cunning;
They have passed the farm already, dear,
    And now they are running.

O where are you going? stay with me here.
   Were the vows you swore me deceiving, deceiving?
No, I promised to love you, dear,
     But I must be leaving.

O it's broken the lock and splintered the door,
   O it's the gate where they're turning, turning;
Their feet are heavy on the floor
     And their eyes are burning.

p. 1934   W. H. AUDEN

Delusions

II

To those who sail the salt quotidian sea
The tempting syren sings across the flood,
But once plunged in, they find her out to be
A desert island with a coast of mud.

Lulled by the waves, no mortal heart resists
The gaudy scenery of the noble bay,
That paradisal image which persists
In all its brightness to the present day.

Each one is Tantalus to what he dreams,
The waters of illusion lap his chin,
Ready to hand the flattering symbol seems
And Tantalus is always taken in.

Each day he starts, he leaps towards the goal,
Driven along by life's impulsive tide.
His wishes are no more in his control
Than the bright objects which his eyes provide.

Boasting each project absolutely new,
His rising sciences, renascent arts,
All that he frames has one grand aim in view,
One which is not declared but simply starts.

Automaton of fate, led on by time,
He learns no lesson from repeated pain.
Like the old lag, he knows the price of crime
And yet he can not help but try again.

Till, one fine day, still hoping against hope
In spite of all this once to be exempt
From nature's warrant and the hangman's rope,
The bourgeois perishes in his attempt.

p. 1936   CHARLES MADGE

Centaurs

The folded land a horse could stamp through
Raised the centaur with lighter hoof.
The glossy vandyke wake of plough

And painted crops were saved: the truth
Is that the centaur did not eat.
The country never set a roof

Among its smoky trees, the sweet
Stables of the centaur lay
Quite open to their augean fate.

What of the land's economy,
Its plans to keep alive the beast,
Whose muscular beauty, white and ghostly,

Stood still against the darker boast?
Being half man it would not draw
The plough or bear the summer harvest:

The other half refused the straw
Shelter, and the elements
Commenced to operate the law.

Clouds covered like a scab the blenched,
Raw sky and from its arching hangar
Slipped bolts that tore the earth to fragments,

Splashing amongst the seething danger
Below the cardboard base the centaur
Had pawed with merely human anger.

c. 1939   ROY FULLER

This Excellent Machine

This excellent machine is neatly planned,
A child, a half-wit would not feel perplexed:
No chance to err, you simply press the button —
At once each cog in motion moves the next,
The whole revolves, and anything that lives
Is quickly sucked towards the running band,
Where, shot between the automatic knives,
It's guaranteed to finish dead as mutton.

This excellent machine will illustrate
The modern world divided into nations:
So neatly planned, that if you merely tap it
The armaments will start their devastations,

And though we're for it, though we're all convinced
Some fool will press the button soon or late,
We stand and stare, expecting to be minced –
And very few are asking *Why not scrap it?*

p. 1932   JOHN LEHMANN

The Caves

This is the cave of which I spoke,
These are the blackened stones, and these
Our footprints, seven lives ago.

Darkness was in the cave like shifting smoke,
Stalagmites grew like equatorial trees,
There was a pool, quite black and silent, seven lives ago.

Here such a one turned back, and there
Another stumbled and his nerve gave out;
Men have escaped blindly, they know not how.

Our candles gutter in the mouldering air,
Here the rock fell, beyond a doubt,
There was no light in those days, and there is none now.

Water drips from the roof, and the caves narrow,
Galleries lead downward to the unknown dark;
This was the point we reached, the farthest known.

Here someone in the debris found an arrow,
Men have been here before, and left their mark
Scratched on the limestone wall with splintered bone.

Here the dark word was said for memory's sake,
And lost, here on the cold sand, to the puzzled brow:

This was the farthest point, the fabled lake:
These were our footprints, seven lives ago.

c. 1939   MICHAEL ROBERTS

Time Was My Friend

I had made Time my hero and my god,
Summer was not complete without his presence.
Slyly fingering the six-guns that dangled at his side,
The bad man of the plains, the man whom posters
Advertised on every stump and broken fence,
I, sick of the intolerance of my masters,
Had made him sheriff in my idle dreams.

He it was who at that final moment
Flicked out his guns and shot away the rope
That tightened on my neck with obvious intent.
In trouble he was always with me, his bright eyes,
His straight sharp nose and his scar-twisted lip
Gave me the courage to spoil the neat surprise
My enemy, the black parson, had planned for me.

My god, my servant, was there at my beck
On his grey horse that had outrun the wind.
With him to cheer me on I always won my trick
For, no matter if my call was bad, I found the ace
I wanted, sprouting in my expectant hand;
At cards no man could see beyond his face.
Time was my hero and I trusted him.

Time was my friend. It served me right,
I never should have given him promotion.
He took advantage and just the other night

He stole the armour I kept against his boisterous jokes,
And when I protested, he, with a careless motion,
As swift and subtle as his own black snakes,
Drew both his guns and shot away my legs.

p. 1939   RUTHVEN TODD

Dictator

From a strange land among the hills, the tall man
Came; who was a cobbler and a rebel at the start
Till he saw power ahead and keenly fought
To seize it; crushed out his comrades then.
His brittle eyes could well outstare the eagle
And the young followed him with cheers and praise
Until, at last, all that they knew – his nights, his days,
His deeds and face were parcel of a fable.

Now in the neat white house that is his home
He rules the flowers and birds just like a king,
And, Napoleon by the sundial, sees his fame
Spread through the garden to the heap of dung;
'All that I do is history,' he loudly cries
Seeing in his shadow his romantic size.

p. 1938   RUTHVEN TODD

The Progress of Poetry

I saw a Gardener with a watering can
Sprinkling dejectedly the heads of men
Buried up to their necks in the wet clay.

I saw a Bishop born in sober black
With a bewildered look on his small face
Being rocked in a cradle by a grey-haired woman.

I saw a man, with an air of painful duty,
Binding his privates up with bunches of ribbon.
The woman who helped him was decently veiled in white.

I said to the Gardener: 'When I was a younger poet
At least my reference to death had some sonority.
I sang the danger and the deeps of love.

Is the world poxy with a fresh disease?
Or is this a maggot I feel here, gnawing my breast
And wrinkling my five senses like a walnut's kernel?'

The Gardener answered: 'I am more vexed by the lichen
Upon my walls. I scraped it off with a spade.
As I did so I heard a very human scream.

'In evening's sacred cool, among my bushes
A Figure was wont to walk. I deemed it angel.
But look at the footprint. There's hair between the toes!'

p. 1939   CHRISTOPHER CAUDWELL

God the Holy Ghost

The well-advertised and too-familiar god
Lived for a long time in the orange grove,
Seen only by reporters who would brave
The ten snakes that were his temple-guard.
As he was news, the papers built his fame,
Told how he cured with one swift acid glance
Or, with another, spoiled a sword's menace;
But no man in all the land could find his name –

Until that day, still spoken of in whispers,
When an old man came crashing from the wood,
Blind as a ghost but far too like his pictures
To be another. For a long pause they stood,
Eyes awed, before fear took them and they ran
Seeing the snakes harmless and their god a man.

p. 1938   RUTHVEN TODD

The Disused Temple

After the scourging prophet, with his cry
Of 'money-changers' and 'my father's house',
Had set his mark upon it, folk were shy
To enter, and the fane fell in disuse.

Since it was unfrequented, and left out
Of living, what was there to do except
Make fast the door, destroy the key? (No doubt
One of our number did it while we slept.)

It stays as a disquieting encumbrance.
We moved the market-place out of its shade,
But still it overhangs our whole remembrance,
Making us both inquisitive and afraid.

Shrewd acousticians hammer on the door
And study from the echoes what is there.
The Röntgen rays with which others explore
Are vain – the photographic plate is bare.

Disquiet makes us sleepy. Shoddiness
Has come upon our crafts. No questions that
We'll shortly have to yield to our distress,
Abandon the whole township, and migrate.

p. 1934   NORMAN CAMERON

Apotheosis of Hero

Sometimes, it would seem, the hero got the game,
Beating the spy who used his honoured name
As subtle camouflage for well-laid plots.
Sometimes he became fabulous, a strong legend
That old men told to boys; his good end
Was to die suddenly by swift shots.

Under the white flag as he advanced
They say he stood bravely, never winced
As the first bullet pierced his lungs.
Another tale, however, was spread by spite,
Death by his own hand in cowering fright,
But that never reached the songs.

Whatever was the truth the man is now
The young girls' hero and the schoolboys' motto.
And no rumour spoils his memory.
He is the aim the father gives his son,
The strong individualist who somehow won
While dying before the enemy.

p. 1938   RUTHVEN TODD

The Unfinished Race

No runner clears the final fence,
The laurels have long since gone stale.
They must be a cardboard pretence,
These watchers crowded on the rail
– What reason to stay watching so
To see a race that has no end?
How many centuries ago
The runners came up round the bend?

Always they baulk at this last leap,
And then recoil to try once more.
From pride or custom still they keep
On striving – those once at the fore
Distinguished only from the ruck
By their impressive long run back.

p. 1933   NORMAN CAMERON

Sonnet

Progressing forward to the backward gates
With frequent conquests followed by despairs,
Divided thus and so the Soul repairs
Not to the tabernacle carved with dates
And stuffy with death-quiet, where there waits
Some chance of rediffusion, where a hand
Rises in blessing over this last land,
But to null vacuum, as the wind states.

Or there are pastures somewhere off the track
Patterned with light of *This* and shade of *That*
Where pain and pleasure both alike fall flat . . .
The pilgrimage is weary and the heart
Ticks not so fast as at the giddy start.
Has not the hour arrived for turning back?

p. 1934   DAVID GASCOYNE

A Fable

He went from the harsh tower of words,
Ancestral home of his mad angry god,
Who flung the lightning and laid flat the wood,
Crushing the field-mice and the nestling birds.

He went from the high tower his fathers
Had built for him upon the edge of light;
Thinking things different in the world without
He hoped the cues would come to him from others.

He chose the hard path at the cross-roads,
As younger sons had done for many years,
And aped the men he met, the latest modes,
Until he reached the climax of his fears
And thought he recognized the thorny track;
As well he might. It was the same way back.

c. 1939   RUTHVEN TODD

VIII. FAREWELL CHORUS

The Sunlight on the Garden

The sunlight on the garden
Hardens and grows cold,
We cannot cage the minute
Within its nets of gold,
When all is told
We cannot beg for pardon.

Our freedom as free lances
Advances towards its end;
The earth compels, upon it
Sonnets and birds descend;
And soon, my friend,
We shall have no time for dances.

The sky was good for flying
Defying the church bells
And every evil iron
Siren and what it tells:
The earth compels,
We are dying, Egypt, dying.

And not expecting pardon,
Hardened in heart anew,
But glad to have sat under
Thunder and rain with you,
And grateful too
For sunlight on the garden.

c. 1938   LOUIS MACNEICE

Hiding Beneath the Furze

Hiding beneath the furze as they passed him by,
  He drowned their talk with the noise of his own heart,
And faltering, came at last to the short hot road
  With the flat white cottage under the rowan trees:
And this can never happen, ever again.

Before his fever drowned him, he stumbled in,
  And the old woman rose, and said in the dialect, 'Enter'.
He entered, and drank, and hearing his fever roaring,
  Surrendered himself to its sweating luxuries:
And this can never happen, ever again.

There were bowls of milk, and (after such hunger) bread.
  Here was the night he had longed for on the highway.
Strange, that his horror could dance so gaily in sunlight,
  And rescue and peace be here in the smoky dark:
And this can never happen, ever again.

When he awoke, he found his pursuers had been,
  But the woman had lied, and easily deceived them.
She had never questioned his right – for who so childish
  Could ever do wrong? 'He is my son,' she had said:
And this can never happen, ever again.

The days passed into weeks, and the newspapers came,
  And he saw that the world was safe, and his name un-
    mentioned.
He could return to the towns and his waiting friends,
  The evil captain had fled defeated to Norway:
And this can never happen, ever again.

And this can never happen, ever again.
   He stands on the icy pier and waits to depart,
The town behind him is lightless, his friends are dead,
   The captain will set his spies in his very heart,
And the fever is gone that rocked inside his head.

Autumn 1939   HENRY REED

It was Easier

Now over the map that took ten million years
Of rain and sun to crust like boiler-slag,
The lines of fighting men progress like caterpillars,
Impersonally looping between the leaf and twig.

One half the map is shaded as if by night
Or an eclipse. It is difficult from far away
To understand that a man's booted feet
May grow blistered marching there, or a boy

Die from a bullet. It is difficult to plant
That map with olives, oranges or grapes,
Or to see men alive at any given point,
To see dust-powdered faces or cracked lips.

It is easier to avoid all thought of it
And shelter in the elegant bower of legend,
To dine in dreams with kings, to float
Down the imaginary river, crowds on each hand

Cheering each mention of my favoured name.
It is easier to collect anecdotes, the tall tales
That travellers, some centuries ago, brought home,
Or wisecracks and the drolleries of fools;

It is easier to sail paper-boats on lily-ponds,
To plunge like a gannet in the sheltered sea,
To go walking or to chatter with my friends
Or to discuss the rare edition over tea,

Than to travel in the mind to that place
Where the map becomes reality, where cracks
Are gullies, a bullet more than half-an-inch
Of small newsprint and the shaped grey rocks

Are no longer the property of wandering painters,
A pleasant watercolour for an academic wall,
But cover for the stoat-eyed snipers
Whose aim is fast and seldom known to fail.

It is easier . . . but no, the map has grown
And now blocks out the legends, the sweet dreams
And the chatter. The map has come alive. I hear the moan
Of the black planes and see their pendant bombs.

I can no longer hide in fancy; they'll hunt me out.
That map has mountains and these men have blood;
'Time has an answer!' cries my familiar ghost,
Stirred by explosives from his feather bed.

Time may have answers but the map is here.
Now is the future that I never wished to see.
I was quite happy dreaming and had no fear;
But now, from the map, a gun is aimed at me.

c. 1939   RUTHVEN TODD

Prognosis

Good-bye, Winter,
The days are getting longer,
The tea-leaf in the teacup
Is herald of a stranger.

Will he bring me business
Or will he bring me gladness
Or will he come for cure
Of his own sickness?

With a pedlar's burden
Walking up the garden
Will he come to beg
Or will he come to bargain?

Will he come to pester,
To cringe or to bluster,
A promise in his palm
Or a gun in his holster?

Will his name be John
Or will his name be Jonah
Crying to repent
On the Island of Iona?

Will his name be Jason
Looking for a seaman
Or a mad crusader
Without rhyme or reason?

What will be his message —
War or work or marriage?
News as new as dawn
Or an old adage?

Will he give a champion
Answer to my question
Or will his words be dark
And his ways evasion?

Will his name be Love
And all his talk be crazy?
Or will his name be Death
And his message easy?

Spring 1939   LOUIS MACNEICE

London Rain

The rain of London pimples
The ebony street with white
And the neon-lamps of London
Stain the canals of night
And the park becomes a jungle
In the alchemy of night.

My wishes turn to violent
Horses black as coal –
The randy mares of fancy,
The stallions of the soul –
Eager to take the fences
That fence about my soul.

Across the countless chimneys
The horses ride and across
The country to the channel
Where warning beacons toss,
To a place where God and No-God
Play at pitch and toss.

278

Whichever wins I am happy
For God will give me bliss
But No-God will absolve me
From all I do amiss
And I need not suffer conscience
If the world was made amiss.

Under God we can reckon
On pardon when we fall
But if we are under No-God
Nothing will matter at all,
Adultery and murder
Will count for nothing at all.

So reinforced by logic
As having nothing to lose
My lust goes riding horseback
To ravish where I choose,
To burgle all the turrets
Of beauty as I choose.

But now the rain gives over
Its dance upon the town,
Logic and lust together
Come dimly tumbling down,
And neither God nor No-God
Is either up or down.

The argument was wilful,
The alternatives untrue,
We need no metaphysics
To sanction what we do
Or to muffle us in comfort
From what we did not do.

Whether the living river
Began in bog or lake,
The world is what was given,
The world is what we make.
And we only can discover
Life in the life we make.

So let the water sizzle
Upon the gleaming slates,
There will be sunshine after
When the rain abates
And rain returning duly
When the sun abates.

My wishes now come homeward,
Their gallopings in vain,
Logic and lust are quiet
And again it starts to rain;
Falling asleep I listen
To the falling London rain.

July 1939   LOUIS MACNEICE

September 1, 1939

I sit in one of the dives
On Fifty-Second Street
Uncertain and afraid
As the clever hopes expire
Of a low dishonest decade:
Waves of anger and fear
Circulate over the bright
And darkened lands of the earth,
Obsessing our private lives;
The unmentionable odour of death
Offends the September night.

Accurate scholarship can
Unearth the whole offence
From Luther until now
That has driven a culture mad,
Find what occurred at Linz,
What huge imago made
A psychopathic god:
I and the public know
What all schoolchildren learn,
Those to whom evil is done
Do evil in return.

Exiled Thucydides knew
All that a speech can say
About Democracy,
And what dictators do,
The elderly rubbish they talk
To an apathetic grave;
Analysed all in his book,
The enlightenment driven away,
The habit-forming pain
Mismanagement and grief:
We must suffer them all again.

Into this neutral air
Where blind skyscrapers use
Their full height to proclaim
The strength of Collective Man,
Each language pours its vain
Competitive excuse:
But who can live for long
In an euphoric dream;
Out of the mirror they stare,
Imperialism's face
And the international wrong.

Faces along the bar
Cling to their average day:
The lights must never go out,
The music must always play,
All the conventions conspire
To make this fort assume
The furniture of home;
Lest we should see where we are,
Lost in a haunted wood,
Children afraid of the night
Who have never been happy or good.

The windiest militant trash
Important Persons shout
Is not so crude as our wish:
What mad Nijinsky wrote
About Diaghilev
Is true of the normal heart;
For the error bred in the bone
Of each woman and each man
Craves what it cannot have,
Not universal love
But to be loved alone.

From the conservative dark
Into the ethical life
The dense commuters come,
Repeating their morning vow;
'I *will* be true to the wife,
I'll concentrate more on my work.'
And helpless governors wake
To resume their compulsory game:
Who can release them now,
Who can reach the deaf,
Who can speak for the dumb?

All I have is a voice
To undo the folded lie,
The romantic lie in the brain
Of the sensual man-in-the-street
And the lie of Authority
Whose buildings grope the sky:
There is no such thing as the State
And no one exists alone;
Hunger allows no choice
To the citizen or the police;
We must love one another or die.

Defenceless under the night
Our world in stupor lies;
Yet, dotted everywhere,
Ironic points of light
Flash out wherever the Just
Exchange their messages:
May I, composed like them
Of Eros and of dust,
Beleaguered by the same
Negation and despair,
Show an affirming flame.

p. 1939   W. H. AUDEN

Farewell Chorus

I

And so! the long black pullman is at last departing, now,
After those undermining years of angry waiting and cold
  tea;
And all your small grey faces and wet hankies slide away
Backwards into the station's cave of cloud. And so Good-bye

To our home-town, so foreign now its lights no longer show;
And to old lives already indistinct as a dull play
We saw while staying somewhere in the Midlands long ago.

Farewell both to the few and to the many; for tonight
Our souls may be required of us; and so we say Adieu
To those who charmed us with their ever ready wit
But could not see the point; to those whose polished hands
And voices could allay a little while our private pain
But could not stay to soothe us when worse bouts began;
To those whose beauties were too brief: Farewell, dear
    friends.

To you as well whom we could never love, hard though
We tried, because our pity told us you were weak,
And whom because of pity we abhorred; to you
Whose gauche distress and badly-written postcards made us
    ache
With angrily impatient self-reproach; you who were too
Indelicately tender, whose too soft eyes made us look
(Against our uncourageous wish) swiftly away . . .

To those, too, whom we hardly knew, or could not know;
To the indifferent and the admired; to the once-met
And long-remembered faces: Yes, Good-bye to you
Who made us turn our heads to look again, and wait
Four hours in vain at the same place next day;
Who for a moment might have been the lost selves sought
Without avail, and whom we know we never shall find now.

Away, away! Yet now it is no longer in retreat
That we are leaving. All our will is drowned
As by an inner tidal-wave that has washed our regret
And small fears and exhausted implications out of mind.
You can't accompany our journey. Nor may we return
Except in unimpassioned recollection from beyond
That ever-nearer frontier that our fate has drawn.

And so let's take a last look-round, and say Farewell to all
Events that gave the last decade, which this New Year
Brings to its close, a special pathos. Let us fill
One final fiery glass and quickly drink to 'the Pre-War'
Before we greet 'the Forties', whose unseen sphinx-face
Is staring fixedly upon us from behind its veil;
Drink farewell quickly, ere the Future smash the glass.

Even while underneath the floor are whirling on
The wheels which carry us towards some Time-to-Come,
Let us perform this hasty mental rite (as one
Might cast a few imagined bays into the tomb
Of an unloved but memorable great man);
Soon the still-near will seem remotely far: there's hardly
   time
For much oration more than mere Good-bye, again:

To the delusive peace of those disintegrating years
Through which burst uncontrollably into our view
Successive and increasingly premonitory flares,
Explosions of the dangerous truth beneath, which no
Steel-plated self-deception could for long withstand . . .
Years through the rising storm of which somehow we grew,
Struggling to keep an anchored heart and open mind,

Too often failing. Years through which none the less
The coaxing of complacency and sleep could still persuade
Kind-hearted Christians of the permanence of Peace,
Increase of common-sense and civic virtue. Years which
   bade
Less placid conscientious souls indignantly arise
Upon ten thousand platforms to proclaim the system mad
And urge the liquidation of a senile ruling-class.
Years like a prison-wall, frustrating though unsound,

On which the brush of History, with quick, neurotic strokes,
Its latest and most awe-inspiring fresco soon outlined:
Spenglerian lowering of the Western skies, red lakes
Of civil bloodshed, free flags flagrantly torn down
By order of macabre puppet orators, the blind
Leading blindfolded followers into the Devil's den . . .

3

And so, Good-bye, grim 'Thirties. These your closing days
Have shown a new light, motionless and far
And clear as ice, to our sore riddled eyes;
And we see certain truths now, which the fear
Aroused by earlier circumstances could but compromise,
Concerning all men's lives. Beyond despair
May we take wiser leave of you, knowing disasters' cause.

Having left all false hopes behind, may we move on
At a vertiginous unmeasured speed, beyond, beyond,
Across this unknown Present's bleak and rocky plain:
Through sudden tunnels; in our ears the wind
Echoing unintelligible guns. Mirrored within
Each lonely consciousness, War's world seems without end.
Dumbly we stare up at strange skies with each day's dawn.

Could you but hear our final farewell call, how strained
And hollow it would sound! We are already far
Away, forever leaving further leagues behind
Of this most perilous and incoherent land
We're in. The unseen enemy are near.
Above the cowering capital Death's wings impend.
Rapidly under ink-black seas today's doomed disappear.

We are alone with one another, but our eyes
Meet seldom in the dark. What a relentless roar
Stuffs every ear, as though with wool! The winds that rise

Out of our dereliction's vortex, hour by hour,
To bring us word of the incessant wordless guns,
Tirades of the insane, thick hum of 'planes, the rage of fire,
Eruptions, waves: all end in utmost silence in our brains.
'The silence after the viaticum.' So silent is the ray
Of naked radiance that lights our actual scene,
Leading the gaze into the nameless and unknown
Extremes of this existence where fear's armour falls away
And lamentation and defeat and pain
Are all transfigured by acceptance; where men see
The tragic splendour of their final destiny.

New Year 1940   DAVID GASCOYNE

Index of Authors

Kenneth Allott (b. 1912)

    Offering (p. 1936), 213
    Prize for Good Conduct (p. 1936), 140
    Lament for a Cricket Eleven (p. 1938), 112
    The Children (w. 1939), 52

W. H. Auden (b. 1907)

    Poems, XXX ('Sir, no man's enemy...') (c. 1930), 201
    Poems, XII ('We made all possible preparations...')
      (c. 1930), 86
    A Communist to Others ('Comrades who when the
      sirens roar...) (p. 1933), 54
    Ballad (p. 1934), 259
    The Witnesses (p. 1933), 249
    To a Writer on His Birthday (p. 1935), 167
    The Dream (p. 1936), 190
    May With Its Light Behaving (c. 1936), 203
    O For Doors to be Open (c. 1936), 70
    Spain (c. 1937), 133
    Song for the New Year (p. 1937), 47
    Lay Your Sleeping Head (p. 1937), 191
    September 1, 1939 (p. 1939), 280

George Barker (b. 1913)

    Resolution of Dependence (p. 1937), 186
    Elegy on Spain (p. 1939), 155

Julian Bell (1908–37)

    Nonsense (p. 1938), 62

John Betjeman (b. 1906)

    Death in Leamington (c. 1932), 121
    Distant View of a Provincial Town (c. 1937), 172
    Slough (c. 1937), 74

Death of King George V (c. 1937), 115
In Westminster Abbey (c. 1940), 127
On a Portrait of a Deaf Man (c. 1940), 118

Ronald Bottrall (b. 1906)
Epitaph for a Riveter (p. 1933), 119

Norman Cameron (1905–53)
The Unfinished Race (p. 1933), 268
No Remedy (p. 1933), 202
Public House Confidence (p. 1933), 127
The Disused Temple (p. 1934), 267
The Compassionate Fool (p. 1934), 257
Forgive me, Sire (p. 1935), 173
In the Queen's Room (p. 1936), 194
To a Greedy Lover (p. 1936), 193

Christopher Caudwell (1907–37)
The Progress of Poetry (p. 1939), 265

John Cornford (1915–36)
A Letter from Aragon (w. 1936), 151
Full Moon at Tierz (w. 1936), 137
To Margot Heinemann (w. 1936), 146

Hugh Sykes Davies
From *Petron* ('A spider weaves ...') (c. 1935), 226
From *Petron* ('In the midst of a ravaged city ...')
  (c. 1935), 226
Poem ('In the stump of the old tree ...') (p. 1936), 227

Clifford Dyment (b. 1914)
The Pharos (c. 1935), 188

William Empson (b. 1906)
This Last Pain (p. 1932), 198
Homage to the British Museum (c. 1935), 200
To an Old Lady (c. 1935), 117
Missing Dates (c. 1940), 73
Just a Smack at Auden (p. 1937), 64

Aubade (c. 1940), 194
Reflection from Anita Loos (c. 1940), 184

Gavin Ewart (b. 1915)
Audenesque for an Initiation (p. 1933), 67

Edgar Foxall
A Note on Working-Class Solidarity (p. 1933), 66
Poem ('He awoke from dreams . . .') (c. 1938), 142
Sea Dirge (c. 1938), 129

Roy Fuller (b. 1912)
End of a City (c. 1939), 255
Centaurs (c. 1939), 261

David Gascoyne (b. 1916)
Morning Dissertation (p. 1933), 222
And the Seventh Dream is the Dream of Isis (p. 1933), 229
Sonnet (p. 1934), 269
The Very Image (p. 1936), 234
Figure in a Landscape (c. 1938), 218
Farewell Chorus (w. 1940), 283

Geoffrey Grigson (b. 1905)
Reginal Order (p. 1933), 116
Before a Fall (p. 1936), 224
The Non-Interveners (w. 1937), 142
Three Evils (p. 1936), 223
And Forgetful of Europe (p. 1938), 125

Bernard Gutteridge (b. 1916)
Home Revisited (p. 1939), 104

Robert Hamer
Torch Song (p. 1934), 88

Rayner Heppenstall (b. 1911)
Risorgimento (p. 1933), 217

Peter Hewitt (b. 1914)
Place of Birth (c. 1939), 102

Laurie Lee (b. 1914)

Music in a Spanish Town (w. 1936), 152
Words Asleep (w. 1936), 153
A Moment of War (w. 1937), 149

John Lehmann (b. 1907)

This Excellent Machine (p. 1932), 262

C. Day Lewis (b. 1904)

From Feathers to Iron, 14 (c. 1931), 100
The Magnetic Mountain, 20 (p. 1933), 63
The Magnetic Mountain, 24 (c. 1933), 204
The Magnetic Mountain, 25 (c. 1933), 61
The Magnetic Mountain, 32 (p. 1933), 49
The Conflict (p. 1933), 199
A Carol (c. 1935), 113
Newsreel (c. 1938), 69
The Bells that Signed (c. 1938), 85

Louis MacNeice (1907–63)

Poem ('Among these turf-stacks . . .') (p. 1933), 98
An Eclogue for Christmas (p. 1934), 205
Birmingham (p. 1934), 80
Bagpipe Music (p. 1938), 72
The Sunlight on the Garden (c. 1938), 273
Autumn Journal, III (c. 1939), 45
Autumn Journal, VI (c. 1939), 160
Autumn Journal, XV (c. 1939), 170
Prognosis (w. 1939), 277
Christina (w. 1939), 256
London Rain (w. 1939), 278
Meeting Point (w. 1939), 192
The British Museum Reading Room (w. 1939), 124

Charles Madge (b. 1912)

Instructions, V (p. 1933), 83
The Times (p. 1933), 139
Delusions, II (p. 1932), 260

H. B. Mallalieu (b. 1914)

Two Preludes (p. 1937), 87
Lament for a Lost Life (p. 1939), 174

Philip O'Connor (b. 1916)

'Blue Bugs in Liquid Silk' (p. 1937), 223
Poems (Captain Busby . . .) (p. 1937), 242
Useful Letter (p. 1938), 232
Poem (The clock ticks on . . .) (p. 1938), 215

Clere Parsons (1908–31)

Different (c. 1932), 70

Geoffrey Parsons (b. 1910)

Suburban Cemetery (w. 1937), 178
Europe a Wood (w. 1938), 99
The Inheritor (w. 1938), 258

F. T. Price (b. 1912)

The Token (c. 1938), 115
An Epistle to a Patron (c. 1938), 179

John Pudney (b. 1909)

Resort (w. 1934), 116

Henry Reed (b. 1914)

Hiding Beneath the Furze (w. 1939), 274

Anne Ridler (b. 1912)

Aisholt Revisited (w. 1939), 106
Zennor (w. 1939), 95
At Richmond (w. 1939), 83

Michael Roberts (1902–48)

The Secret Springs (c. 1936), 95
In Our Time (c. 1939), 53
The Child (c. 1939), 114
The Caves (c. 1939), 263

Roger Roughton (1916–41)

Lady Windermere's Fan-Dance (p. 1936), 240
Animal Crackers in Your Croup (p. 1936), 239
Soluble Noughts and Crosses (p. 1936), 235

Francis Scarfe (b. 1911)

Progression (c. 1940), 84
Beauty, Boloney (p. 1939), 76

John Short (b. 1911)

Carol (p. 1936), 114

Bernard Spencer (b. 1909)

Evasions (p. 1935), 183
A Thousand Killed (p. 1936), 141
Allotments: April (p. 1936), 105
A Cold Night (p. 1937), 143
Part of Plenty (p. 1937), 123

Stephen Spender (b. 1909)

The Express (p. 1932), 79
I Think Continually (c. 1933), 111
The Landscape Near an Aerodrome (c. 1933), 82
The Pylons (c. 1933), 99
New Year (p. 1934), 90
Fall of a City (c. 1939), 154
Port Bou (c. 1939), 146
Two Armies (c. 1939), 144
An Elementary School Class Room (c. 1939), 51
Thoughts During an Air Raid (c. 1939), 150
Easter Monday (p. 1935), 89
Ultima Ratio Regum (c. 1939), 148

Randall Swingler (b. 1909)

From *The New World This Hour Begets* (c. 1933)
Request for the Day (c. 1933), 189
In Death the Eyes are Still (p. 1934), 202

Julian Symons (b. 1912)

Poem ('If truth can still be told . . .') (p. 1937), 188

INDEX OF AUTHORS

Dylan Thomas (1914–53)

   I see the Boys of Summer (p. 1934), 237
   Light Breaks Where No Sun Shines (c. 1934), 221
   The Force that Through the Green Fuse (c. 1934), 228
   And Death Shall Have No Dominion (c. 1936), 216
   I Have Longed to Move Away (p. 1935), 185
   Should Lanterns Shine (p. 1935), 241
   The Hand that Signed the Paper (p. 1935), 153
   In Memory of Ann Jones (c. 1939), 122
   Twenty-four Years Remind the Tears of my Eyes (c. 1939), 225

Ruthven Todd (b. 1914)

   Worm Interviewed (p. 1936), 215
   In September (p. 1938), 97
   It Was Easier (c. 1939), 275
   Dictator (p. 1938), 265
   Apotheosis of Hero (p. 1938), 268
   God the Holy Ghost (p. 1938), 266
   A Fable (c. 1939), 269
   Time Was My Friend (p. 1939), 264

Rex Warner (b. 1905)

   Hymn (p. 1933), 59
   Sonnet ('The brightness, the peculiar splendour ...') (p. 1935), 89
   Sonnet ('How sweet only to delight lambs ...') (c. 1937), 101
   Light and Air (c. 1937), 176

Vernon Watkins (b. 1906)

   The Collier (w. 1937-8), 119
   Elegy on the Heroine of Childhood (w. 1939), 196

Index of Titles

Aisholt Revisited   106
Allotments: April   105
And Death Shall Have No Dominion   216
And Forgetful of Europe   125
And the Seventh Dream is the Dream of Isis   229
Animal Crackers in Your Croup   239
Apotheosis of Hero   268
At Richmond   83
Aubade   194
Audenesque for an Initiation   67
Autumn Journal III   45
Autumn Journal VI   160
Autumn Journal XV   170

Bagpipe Music   72
Ballad   259
Beauty, Boloney   76
Before a Fall   224
Bells that Signed, The   85
Birmingham   80
'Blue Bugs in Liquid Silk'   223
British Museum Reading Room, The   124

Carol   114
Carol, A   113
Caves, The   263
Centaurs   261
Child, The   114
Children, The   52
Christina   256
Cold Night, A   143
Collier, The   119
Communist to Others, A   54

Compassionate Fool, The   257
Conflict, The   199

Death in Leamington   121
Death of King George V   115
Delusions II   260
Dictator   265
Different   70
Distant View of a Provincial Town   172
Disused Temple, The   267
Dream, The   190

Easter Monday   89
Eclogue for Christmas, An   205
Elegy on Spain   155
Elegy on the Heroine of Childhood   196
Elementary School Class Room, An   51
End of a City   255
Epistle to a Patron, An   179
Epitaph for a Riveter   119
Europe a Wood   99
Evasions   183
Express, The   79

Fable, A   269
Fall of a City   154
Farewell Chorus   283
Figure in a Landscape   218
Force that Through the Green Fuse, The   228
Forgive me, Sire   173
From Feathers to Iron, 14   100
Full Moon at Tierz   137

God the Holy Ghost   226

Hand that Signed the Paper, The   153
Hiding Beneath the Furze   274
Homage to the British Museum   200
Home Revisited   104
Hymn   59

I Have Longed to Move Away   185
I see the Boys of Summer   237
I Think Continually   111
In Death the Eyes are Still   202
In Memory of Ann Jones   122
In Our Time   53
In September   97
In the Queen's Room   194
In Westminster Abbey   127
Inheritor, The   258
Instructions, V   83
It was Easier   275

Just a Smack at Auden   64

Lady Windermere's Fan-Dance   240
Lament for a Cricket Eleven   112
Lament for a Lost Life   174
Landscape near an Aerodrome, The   82
Lay Your Sleeping Head   191
Letter from Aragon, A   151
London Rain   278
Light and Air   176
Light Breaks Where No Sun Shines   221

Magnetic Mountain 20, The   63
Magnetic Mountain 24, The   204
Magnetic Mountain 25, The   61
Magnetic Mountain 32, The   49
May with its Light Behaving   203
Meeting Point   192
Missing Dates   73
Moment of War, A   149
Morning Dissertation   222
Music in a Spanish Town   152

New Year   90
Newsreel   69
Non-Interveners, The   142

Nonsense   62
No Remedy   202
Note on Working-Class Solidarity, A   66

Offering   213
O for Doors to be Open   70
On a Portrait of a Deaf Man   118

Part of Plenty   123
Petron, from ('A spider weaves . . .')   226
Petron, from ('In the midst . . .')   226
Pharos, The   188
Place of Birth   102
Poem ('Among these turf-stacks . . .')   98
Poem ('He awoke from dreams . . .')   142
Poem ('If truth can still be told . . .')   188
Poem ('In the stump of the old tree . . .') 227
Poem ('The clock ticks on . . .')   215
Poems ('Captain Busby . . .')   242
Poems, XII   86
Poems, XXX   201
Port Bou   146
Prize for Good Conduct   140
Prognosis   277
Progress of Poetry, The   265
Progression   84
Public-House Confidence   127
Pylons, The,   99

Reflection from Anita Loos   184
Reginal Order   116
Request for the Day   189
Resolution of Dependence   186
Resort   116
Risorgimento   217

Sea Dirge   129
Secret Springs, The   95
September 1, 1939,   280
Should Lanterns Shine   241

Slough	74
Soluble Noughts and Crosses	235
Song for the New Year	47
Sonnet ('How sweet only to delight lambs . . .')	101
Sonnet ('Progressing forward to the backward gates . . .')	269
Sonnet ('The brightness, the peculiar splendour . . .')	89
Spain	133
Suburban Cemetery	178
Sunlight on the Garden, The	273
The New World This Hour Begets, XI	77
This Excellent Machine	262
This Last Pain	198
Thoughts During an Air Raid	150
Thousand Killed, A	141
Three Evils	223
Time Was My Friend	264
Times, The	139
To a Greedy Lover	193
To a Writer on His Birthday	167
To an Old Lady	117
To Margot Heinemann	146
Token, The	115
Torch Song	88
Twenty-four Years Remind the Tears of My Eyes	225
Two Armies	144
Two Preludes	87
Ultima Ratio Regum	148
Unfinished Race, The	268
Useful Letter	232
Very Image, The	234
Witnesses, The	249
Words Asleep	153
Worm Interviewed	215
Zennor	95

MORE ABOUT PENGUINS
AND PELICANS

For further information about books available from
Penguins please write to Dept EP, Penguin Books Ltd,
Harmondsworth, Middlesex UB7 ODA.

In the U.S.A.: For a complete list of books available
from Penguins in the United States write to Dept CS,
Penguin Books, 625 Madison Avenue, New York,
New York 10022.

In Canada: For a complete list of books available from
Penguins in Canada write to Penguin Books Canada
Ltd, 2801 John Street, Markham, Ontario L3R 1B4.

In Australia: For a complete list of books available
from Penguins in Australia write to the Marketing
Department, Penguin Books Australia Ltd, P.O. Box
257, Ringwood, Victoria 3134.